A JOURNALIST'S JOURNEY
WRITINGS OF A HALL OF FAME NEWSPAPERMAN

RAYMOND MOSCOWITZ

All rights reserved. No part of this book may be reproduced in any way or by any means without the express written permission of the publisher.

Copyright ©2013 by Raymond Moscowitz

>Published by:
>Life Sentences Publishing
>434 Kentucky Avenue
>Tipton, Indiana 46072
>LifeSentencesPublishing@aol.com
>(765) 437-0149

Dedication

To the memory of Basil L. "Stuffy" Walters,
who paved the way.

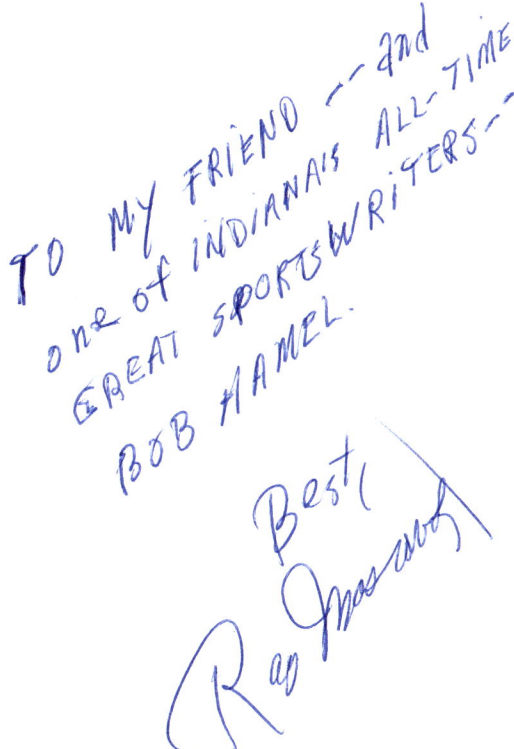

Acknowledgements

Permission to reprint the news stories, features, editorials and columns in this book has been granted from these newspaper companies:

- Paxton Media Group of Paducah, Ky., which acquired Nixon Newspapers, Inc. in 1998.
- Cox Ohio Publishing, based in Dayton, Ohio.
- The Journal Gazette of Fort Wayne, Ind.

The manuscript was prepared for publication by Janis Thornton of Life Sentences Publishing, based in Tipton, Ind.

This book would not have been possible without the work of the author's wife, Barbara Moscowitz, who preserved copies of everything he wrote during his career.

Contents

Preface	1
1. GOP senatorial candidate charges 'fear campaign'	5
2. Reporter tells ordeal on emergency vehicle	8
3. Spiritual medicine turns junkie to man of faith	12
4. Blaze Destroys Burlap Plant	16
5. He Seeks Trouble, Usually Finds It	19
6. Ever Want To Join Circus? JH Reporter Did For Day	24
7. London action moves along Kings Road	27
8. Night callers	30
9. Love Nibbles at Dwindling Lithuanian Clan	34
10. Nolan, Zipperian contracts deny Kays 2 appointments	38
11. GOP blood flows in Clinton County	42
12. De facto secrecy	46
13. Lights dim, sounds blast — Matt rolls	48
14. Bowen, Bulen in 10-second drama	51
15. Gas strike not for him, but...	54
16. Egyptians stress impact of 'new' Suez Canal	57
17. HRC — people, love, rebirth	61
18. A Christmas that tops them all	64
19. 'America's most trusted man' speaks his mind	67
20. 'Music is endless,' Goodman says — and he should know	72
21. Sen. Bayh bids farewell to Oval Office goal	75
22. Life's facets no stranger to treaty negotiator	79
23. Is Dan Quayle the man to beat Bayh? He's not saying, but then again	83
24. Modern health care is real question	88
25. Remember Jim Neal, GOP party healer?	90
26. Road to SALT dotted with minefields	94

27. Ruckelshaus: We're still suffering from Watergate 98
28. Lugar tells executives he wants to hold SALT aces 102
29. Professor wary of warlike mood 106
30. Willkie's steamy return to Elwood 110
31. English professor wages battle on censorship 117
32. The Battle for Chicago 122
33. Bobby Knight is complex and misunderstood 138
34. Memories of pancakes, pot pies, simple joys 144
35. A little less arrogance, a little more credibility 147
36. Don't underestimate Richard Nixon's savvy, skill 151
37. GenCorp: A time to talk 156
38. Tragedy sears our senses, too 159
39. Learning the hard way 162
40. When a child grabs our hearts 164
41. Reflections emerge as 50 arrives 166
42. Buckeye Bound and Beyond 170
43. Consolidation: where we stand 180
44. Noble proves you can go home again 183
45. Highway of cooperation 189
46. Indy: The Most Adequate Spectacle in Racing? 195
47. Steel firm's dynamo 201
48. Cobbler is sole survivor 209
49. Debate rages as area jobs feel
    effects of widening economy 214
50. Bulldog rises from ashes with city's help 222

Preface

For more than 60 years I have been a news junkie, starting as a kid in St. Louis who thoroughly read the sports pages of the *Post-Dispatch* and the *Globe-Democrat* every day.

When I was 10, my family moved to Los Angeles. I began to read the L.A. papers — and not just sports — the *Times, Examiner, Herald, Mirror* and the *Daily News*. Eventually, the *Daily News* folded, the Chandler-owned *Mirror* was merged into the *Times*, and the Hearst-owned *Examiner* was merged into the *Herald*. There was still plenty of print to feast on.

As a 10th grader at Hamilton High School, I joined the weekly school newspaper, *The Federalist*, to cover sports. After a few weeks, the adviser told me I had writing ability, so I set a goal to become a sportswriter.

But my curiosity about life in general overwhelmed my love of sports. I decided that I wanted to become a general news reporter. I achieved that goal and much more as a newspaperman, which gave me the opportunity to write about a wide range of subjects and an eclectic collection of people.

That's the context for this book, the essence of which is to portray the evolution of a grassroots journalist over five decades.

After getting my degree in journalism at Los Angeles State College (now University), I spent 14 months as editor of a nationwide political monthly for college students. Then I moved on to my first job on a daily newspaper — a move that took me from Los Angeles, population around 2,000,000, to Frankfort, Ind., population 15,000. I was the only reporter on the five-person *Frankfort Morning Times* staff.

After 17 months, my journalistic godfather, Basil L. "Stuffy"

Walters, arranged interviews for me at larger newspapers. Walters had retired to his native Frankfort after a highly acclaimed newspaper career that included being editor of the *Chicago Daily News* and of Knight Newspapers.

Through Stuffy, I accepted a position in a management program with the *Dayton Journal Herald* in 1965. That program exposed me to all facets of the newsroom. After almost two years, I became an assistant city editor. Government, politics, education, health care, and people became uppermost in mind, both professionally and personally.

In 1969, the *Frankfort Morning Times* was sold to the Nixon family, whose small group of newspapers was based in Wabash, Ind. Tom Heth, who represented the Fowler family that owned the paper, put me in contact with Joe Nixon, who was president of Nixon Newspapers Associates at the time.

After being interviewed by Joe and the paper's new associate publisher, John Mitchell, I was hired as managing editor. It would be the start of a 29-year career with what would become Nixon Newspapers, Inc. (NNI), before I retired in June 1998.

After retiring, I taught classes at Indiana University-Kokomo, worked as a writing coach, consulted for newspapers and wrote freelance articles, primarily for the Fort Wayne *Journal Gazette*.

That evolution as an observer of events occurred smoothly and naturally for me, in large part because of tremendous opportunities I received during almost three decades with Nixon Newspapers, Inc.

Joe Nixon and his younger half-brother, John, who eventually became CEO, loved newspapers. So did John Mitchell, who eventually became NNI's executive vice president and chief operating officer. They believed in newspapers as public trusts. And they thought big, which afforded me and others who worked for NNI to report and write about major issues. The Nixons and Mitchell made sure that NNI earned a healthy profit. Without it, idealism overtakes realism. But they were not driven by profit; they were driven by quality, which, in the final analysis, drives profit.

I later became the editor of NNI's flagship newspaper, the *News Dispatch*, in Michigan City, Ind., and, at the same time, served as executive editor of NNI's 12 newspapers. After Michigan City, I had rewarding stints as publisher of the *Wabash Plain Dealer* and the *Peru Tribune*. I spent the last 10 years at NNI as editorial director, overseeing the news departments of the company's 12 newspapers. Along the way, I wrote two books. I have never stopped writing from the time I became seriously engaged at Hamilton High School.

THERE'S A SENSE OF HISTORY in *A Journalist's Journey* — a natural byproduct, rather than a primary goal in selecting 50 pieces of writing from several hundred.
There's a feature on how Carnaby Street in London, which was the rage in cultural circles in the mid 1960s, appeared to be giving way to King's Road as signs of class disintegration in England were becoming apparent. The feature story was part of a 14-piece series I wrote in 1967 for the Dayton *Journal Herald*.
There's a column on spiking gas prices in the early 1970s causing economic hardship, bringing to mind the old expression, "The more things change, the more they stay the same." (Actually, that expression comes to mind often while reading these pieces.) I wrote the column on gas prices as managing editor in Frankfort.
There's a story about Egypt in the wake of the 1973 October War, written from Cairo. The piece is part of a 14-part series I wrote for Nixon Newspapers, which sent me to the Middle East in the spring of 1974 as part of a press tour sponsored by several media organizations.
There's background and insight on the Panama Canal treaties in a profile on chief negotiator Sol Linowitz. I wrote that piece for the Nixon Hoosier Feature Service that I had created.
There's light shed on the Watergate scandal in an interview with Hoosier William Ruckelshaus, who was one of the victims of the "Saturday Night Massacre." That, too, was syndicated by the Nixon feature service.
There's a chapter from my first book, a biography of Basil Walters. And there's a chapter from my second book, *Small School, Giant Dream: A Year of Hoosier High School Hoopla*, the true story of a small Indiana high school.

There are editorials on important issues that occurred in Frankfort, Wabash and Peru, three of the four towns in which I served NNI as editor and/or publisher.

There's an in-depth exploration of how globalization was inexorably changing the world's economies as a new century was unfolding. I wrote the piece as part of a series for the Fort Wayne *Journal Gazette*.

There's an emphasis on government and politics, because they were central to my career as a reporter, editor and corporate editorial director. But there are several pieces on people, some major figures at times, others every-day folk who were interesting and fascinating in their own ways.

You will note that there are different styles in dates, addresses, titles, and related matters. I chose to replicate the original text as closely as I could. Many pieces were published in more than one newspaper. I used the headline in the newspaper where the piece originated. And you will note that the *Frankfort Morning Times* becomes the *Frankfort Times*, which occurred in the spring of 1971, when the newspaper switched to afternoon publication.

Journalism has been described as "the first rough draft of history." I hope that *A Journalist's Journey* makes a small contribution.

Ray Moscowitz
Bloomington, Indiana
August 2013

GOP senatorial candidate charges 'fear campaign'

Frankfort Morning Times, Sept. 22, 1964

A Journalist's Journey unfolds with this story — a rather routine piece on a U.S. Senate candidate giving a stump speech — because the story became a turning point in my young career. I wrote this story in about 45 minutes on deadline.

The piece drew lavish praise from Basil "Stuffy" Walters, who, after retiring from Knight Newspapers, had settled in at the Clinton County farm on which he had been raised. Walters wrote:

"Dear Ray: You certainly did a splendid objective reporting job on the Bontrager speech. And you proved that objective political reporting can be interesting. If all the reporting in this campaign throughout the nation were equally conscientious, I would not worry about the critics of the press. By such standards, I would award you, sir, with A plus. Best, Stuffy."

That led to a Sunday dinner at Stuffy's home, which turned into a friendship that would play a major role in my career until his death in 1975. I became his biographer in 1982, when the Iowa State University Press published *Stuffy: The Life of Newspaper Pioneer Basil "Stuffy" Walters*.

A weary-appearing D. Russell Bontrager, the Republicans' U.S. Senate nominee, Monday night stung his incumbent foe and claimed the Johnson administration was conducting a campaign of fear in an effort to maintain bureaucratic control.

Speaking before a gathering of 200 people in the auditorium of the Senior High School, Bontrager said the Democrats are "scaring the wits out of you and me so that citizens will lose their objectivity in casting their ballots."

Bontrager, who earlier in the day had delivered about 20 "short talks" in and around Indianapolis, said the present campaign would become the "filthiest, dirtiest campaign of them all."

He cited television commercials which denote that Barry Goldwater is a man of war, not peace, and that the food Americans eat in the future will be safe from Strotium-90, thanks to the test ban treaty, which Goldwater voted against.

The Elkhart attorney called the current Democrat campaign tactics a "most diabolically vicious thing," and he compared the Democrats' methods with that of Hitler in overthrowing the Reichstag.

"Are we going to rip the cloak off these people and expose them for the tyrants they are? Are we going to do that?" Bontrager asked. There was a sprinkling of "yesses" from the audience.

The administration, Bontrager continued, has deeply imbedded fear into the Social Security recipient by saying Goldwater is against the present system. In actuality, the GOP nominee said, Goldwater only wants the system to be more stable.

Bontrager attacked the government's "constant spiraling of debt leading to inflation." The U.S. owes $28 billion more than all of the other nations in the world combined, he said, and as an example he used the purchasing of a bond he bought for his son 22 years ago to show how inflation has cut into the value of the dollar.

Of the current $311.5 billion debt, the Federal government lost $31 billion in grain storage, Bontrager said, pointing out that the farmers' parity is the lowest it has been since 1939.

"Farmers know how to farm," the Republican candidate said, "bureaucrats don't." The government, he added, must phase itself out of the "farming business."

Still on the subject of farming, Bontrager said that in the recently passed poverty bill there was a section — which was eventually deleted — that called for the government buying 200,000 acres and reselling them to 25,000 families in 80-acre sections. If the families couldn't make a go of it, the Federal treasury would pick up the tab, the provision called for.

Bontrager, as lieutenant governor aspirant John M. Ryan mentioned recently at a GOP breakfast, said it is imperative to re-elect

Republicans Walter Sprinkle and Roy Conrad to the State General Assembly for 1965, because, under reapportion rulings handed down by the Supreme Court, the Democrats "will gerrymander us to death" if they get control of the Indiana legislature.

The nominee closed his talk by castigating his opponent, Sen. Vance Hartke, who he referred to as "vacillating Vance from Vanderburgh." Hartke "is nothing more than a White House puppet who will completely reverse himself when the White House pulls his string," Bontrager said.

"If it were not for Senator Hartke," Bontrager said, "the women of Indiana — and the entire nation — no longer would be paying federal excise taxes (on cosmetics, jewelry, furs, etc.).

"And now, only seven months after he voted against repeal of the taxes, he is prancing all over Indiana waving about a campaign brochure in which he promises beginning next January 'to start the battle against these onerous and unfair luxury taxes.'

"He goes on to say in that pamphlet that 'we promised to repeal after the war but we have ignored the obligation.'

"What gall! What double-talk! What just plain lying!"

Hartke, Bontrager said, in a speech on the floor of the Senate, called for abolition of secrecy in government. In that speech, the GOP nominee said, Hartke remarked: "What we are talking about is the right of the individual citizen to have accurate and freely available information about the government."

But on Sept. 10 of this year, when the Senate voted to reopen the Bobby Baker investigation, "the senator must have forgotten his high-sounding words of six months before because he voted — as the administration demanded — against opening the hearing to the public."

Bontrager concluded: "We must seek freedom under the law, not dictatorial bureaucracy."

Reporter tells ordeal on emergency vehicle

Frankfort Morning Times, Feb. 26, 1965

Weather is always a big story. As someone who had grown up mostly in Southern California, I discovered this first-hand some 10 months after joining the *Frankfort Morning Times*, when one of the worst winter storms in decades hit Indiana.
This story uses the first-person and changes tenses. I wondered if my editor, Vance Sappenfield, would heavily edit the piece or ask me to rewrite it. But when he finished reading it, he had a broad grin and said, "Excellent story."

THE LEWIS HARSHMAN FARM, THURSDAY AFTERNOON — Outlined against a dirty blue sky, white powder blasts through the air, obscuring a row of trees about a half mile north.

Gusts up to 60 miles per hour pound away at this farmhouse, where two drivers, an Alcoa employee and a newspaper reporter from California are shown the best in hospitality by Mrs. Lewis (Chloe) Harshman.

The Harshman home, seven miles west of Frankfort on Ind. 28, Thursday became some sort of point of no return as drifts from unyielding snow piled as high as 10 feet.

Mr. Harshman, an employee of the Eli Lilly plant in Lafayette, was due back at 8:30 a.m. Thursday. The snow had stopped him from playing "co-host," and so his 3 1/2-month-old son, Paul, had taken over with an occasional wail.

At 5 a.m., Mrs. Harshman was awakened by Blake Gwinn, who drives a semi-trailer for Daum Overnight Express. Gwinn, of Anderson, has been driving through Frankfort regularly for the last 10 years.

This, he said, was the first time he had to call a halt to his trip.

"I'm not in the habit of doing this (getting women out of bed)," Gwinn chuckled as he held Paul, while Chloe prepared a feeding — two hours behind schedule.

Three hours after Gwinn's arrival, Harold Dyar of Greenfield, pulled up stakes at the Harshman residence, leaving his Kroger semi stranded in the swirling white sand.

Chloe said that she had planned to shop at the Kroger's in Frankfort, only to have the snow change her plans.

"What service," Gwinn said. "Kroger's pulls right up at your door."

Dyar chuckled and reported that his truck, headed for Lafayette, was indeed well-stocked.

He pointed to a couple of loaves of bread and a dozen eggs he snatched from the truck before reaching the warmth and safety of the Harshman home.

* * * * *

At 11 a.m., this reporter had boarded the M-4 amphibious vehicle used by the city's Civil Defense Department.

Along with Rev. Charles Ridlen, Civil Defense Director Herb Switzer, Frankfort fireman Mitch Huff and city policemen Jack Pippenger and Richard Kaylor, we headed for Rossville, to take Huff home. Then we started for Fickle.

The officers had invited me along, specifically to watch a road-clearing operation at Fickle, where stalled vehicles were holding up highway-clearing crews.

I accepted. Kaylor said I would need a hat, got one for me from his locker. The head piece slid neatly over my head and ears. Rev. Ridlen and the others said I didn't have enough clothes, but I dissented, said I'd be okay. Still, I accepted a pair of gloves from the minister.

The journey — now I know how Lewis and Clark must have felt — to Fickle proved to be a chilling episode, no pun intended.

At Jefferson, the M-4 showed its tremendous value by pulling two cars out of the right-of-way. One of the vehicles belonged to Ralph

Galey of Frankfort, who was on his way to Alcoa, only to be stopped from getting to work for the first time in 10 years.

Galey joined us in the M-4 and we trudged on, the wind shooting blasts of broken snowflakes through the tattered plastic windows of the M-4.

After more than two hours in the M-4, piloted expertly by Pippenger, who drove tanks in the Army, we arrived at Harshman's point of no return.

By this time, the M-4 group had encountered Dave Michael of the construction firm bearing his name, plus two of his employees. They were in Michael's truck, headed for the junction of 28 and U.S. 52 to get a caterpillar for road-clearing operations.

The M-4 was needed to drag the truck, which was not gaining much ground in Jefferson. But after a short time, the thick steel chain shattered. It wasn't surprising. At times the M-4 felt like a roller coaster, sliding up and down drifts six to eight feet high.

After warming-up operations at the Harshman home, everyone departed in the M-4, except for the two early arrivals, Galey and this reporter, who by this time had received a bad case of frozen toes.

The two truck drivers, Galey, Mrs. Harshman and yours truly then began a 3-hour discussion that was far-reaching in scope. Paul was a perfect gentleman in his crib.

* * * * *

Now, shortly before 5 p.m., Michael's two men, Rex Swaim and Frank Riley, can be spotted outside with the caterpillar, clearing a path for a flood of cars.

Their job in front of the Harshman home is the toughest as they push snow about 10 feet high in spots.

From the window, Riley can be viewed atop the open caterpillar, while Swaim begins to turn the Michael's truck, long since abandoned, back toward Frankfort.

The icy blasts have chased the two men into the house now for a second time, and Riley, rushing toward the door, has a sunset red face.

A couple of cars inch ahead, going out of sight momentarily as they pass the drifts.

But they'll soon have to wait until Swaim and Riley return to their thankless (paid for or not) task of clearing the way.

This reporter and Galey will board the Michael's truck, while the two truck drivers linger on, hoping to eventually get around the stream of traffic coming east and reach some destination — any destination.

After all, how long can you impose?

A Journalist's Journey

Spiritual Medicine Turns Junkie to Man of Faith

Dayton *Journal Herald*, Dec. 25, 1965

After 17 months in Frankfort, I moved from grassroots journalism, which I loved, to big-city journalism in Dayton, Ohio, where I would hone my skills as a journalist.

I was covering the police beat when I stepped out of the press room on Dec. 23 and nearly bumped into a small, thin, balding man dressed in a natty blue suit.

"Hello, I'm Bill Cuesta," he said with a smile. "My friends call me Sonny."

"Ray Moscowitz with the *Journal Herald*," I responded.

We got into a conversation, and I was taken by what Cuesta told me.

Before returning to the office, I asked the front desk sergeant if he had heard of William Cuesta. Yes, the sergeant said, Cuesta was working with various police units.

I checked Cuesta out. Satisfied that he was for real, I told Tony Svet, an assistant city editor, about him.

"Is he legit?" asked Svet, a veteran newsman.

"Yeah," I replied with a nod.

Svet told me to write the piece for the Christmas-day paper.

The story's initial paragraphs were set in italic type, as shown here.

Your name is William Cuesta — your friends call you Sonny — and you've been a drug addict for 17 years. It is November 1961, and cold seeps through the rags on your body as you sit on a Bronx rooftop. You are about to commit suicide.

You empty seven bags of heroin into a cap from a wine bottle, dissolve the "junk" with water, put a match underneath it. Now you put it into an eyedropper — a makeshift hypodermic needle — and tie a belt around your arm. You find a vein, make the injection.

Your heart immediately reacts, feels as if it is about to jump out of your chest. You stand up and panic, but it is too late. You feel yourself going under, losing consciousness, and you yell, "Oh, God! Help me!"

And He does.

Today, William Cuesta, 5-4, 145 pounds, is a 34-year-old licensed minister who has just joined Youth for Christ in Dayton. He will specialize in preventing juvenile delinquency — and he will do it by recounting experiences similar to the one above.

He will tell young people about when he puffed his first marijuana cigarette at the age of 13 and how, at the age of 16, he participated in the gang slaying of a youth.

And he will talk about his five years in Sing Sing and the withdrawal periods from dope — the hot and cold flashes, the running nose, the excruciating stomach pain, the dank feeling and the coughing up of yellow phlegm.

But most of all, William Cuesta will talk about God.

"What is needed," Cuesta will tell young people, "is love and understanding for the addict. I remember a lot of times when I was deeply addicted. I would find myself in a city as big as New York and having to go to a garbage can for a piece of bread …

"Spiritual medicine … everyone needs it. If the different churches would realize this, more and more drug addicts could kick the habit with spiritual medicine."

It was a church in a "junkie" neighborhood that saved Cuesta. He says he doesn't remember what happened to him after his lethal dose of heroin, only that when he awoke he noticed he wasn't on the rooftop but in a church.

"I don't know how much time elapsed," he recalls. "They found me on the second floor of the mission and took me for dead and called an ambulance. And they prayed while they waited.

"I opened my eyes when I heard them and I felt something different in my life at that moment."

That was at the Bronx's Damascus Christian church, which plays a major role in rehabilitating addicts.

Cuesta says that there he realized his problem was not mental or physical, "but must have been spiritual."

He did not come from a broken home, but his parents "were not faithful Catholics." Addiction had aroused anti-God feelings in him. "I actually idolized heroin, but from the time I awoke, I felt different inwardly ...

"I was afraid to go out into the street after this experience, so the church people started treating me and they bolstered my morale and I began to believe there was a God. All this time I didn't feel the habit."

He spent six months in the church's rehabilitation camp, regained his health and knew that he had to help God. And other addicts.

He worked in 1963 and 1964 for the church in New York, and then early this year began to hold evangelical meetings for the Open Bible Standard churches. In March, he came to Dayton. He says he will be here indefinitely.

That William Cuesta is in Dayton at all is difficult to fathom.

Because during those 17 years of hell before the suicide attempt, there were eight years in prisons, there was an attempt to hang himself, there was the death of his mother, there were constant withdrawal periods — as much as 16 days — and there was the death of a 19-year-old girl addict who died while he was in a jail.

"She (the girl) took an overdose," Cuesta explained. "My family threw me out of the house for stealing from them to support my habit. I lived with her and she prostituted herself to support us."

As for his mother, a victim of cancer, Cuesta noted: "I have to confess that I was void of any emotion or feelings, because of leading such a rotten life." He was in jail, awaiting sentencing to Sing Sing for burglary, when his mother died.

After Sing Sing, where he spent 48 months of a 2-to-5-year term, Cuesta got $20 and fare. He got off at 125th Street in Manhattan, "and the first thing I did was look for narcotics. I was still mentally afflicted, because I had been using 'jailhouse drugs' (a mixture of pills)."

When his family learned that he was stealing from them again, Cuesta once more found himself in the jungle — but this time there was no girl to live with and off of.

Now there were only the rooftops and the garbage cans. "I was a bum." And now it was time for a decision — to either call a halt to that type of existence or to call a halt, period.

That was when Cuesta chose the latter, but God wouldn't let him die.

Blaze Destroys Burlap Plant

Dayton *Journal Herald*, Jan. 22, 1966

Sometimes with a little luck and a lot of ingenuity, reporters are able to write a relatively exclusive initial account of a hard news story.

After getting ready for work one afternoon, I went to my apartment-lobby mailbox.

The couple who managed the complex lived right off the lobby; their door was usually partially open. The husband was a retired Dayton firefighter who still monitored fire runs. As I walked past the door after getting my mail, it swung wide open and the ex-firefighter burst out.

"Hey, listen to this," he said excitedly.

I stepped into the apartment and heard the first call for units to respond to the Kravitz Burlap Bag Company.

"Sounds big," the ex-firefighter said.

"May I use your phone?" I asked.

"Sure," he responded.

I called the city desk, which was not aware of the blaze, and was told to get there pronto. I ran upstairs to my apartment, dropped my mail, grabbed my winter overcoat and sped to the bag plant located in the inner city.

It took only a few minutes to reach the site, but by the time I arrived, thick black smoke was spiraling in the air and traffic was being stopped a block from the plant. I parked and ran to the factory.

My story led the next morning's paper.

A four-story burlap bag company building was destroyed yesterday in a fire which raised clouds of smoke that could be seen all over downtown Dayton. The loss was estimated at $150,000.

A retired assistant fire chief suffered a stroke during the blaze, but there were no injuries directly attributed to the fire at the Kravitz Bag Company, 426 Burns Avenue.

Cause was not determined.

E. J. Wagner, 53, who said he was bailing burlaps and cuttings in the plant, was the first person to notice the flames.

"It started right underneath my feet, and away she went," said Wagner, an employee of the firm for 14 years.

Shelby Jones, 27, said he then walked into the rear of the building and immediately started warning other employees. "We got out of there fast," Jones said.

He said he called to Don Messer, another employee, who then called the fire department.

Willie Dennis, 19, said he was in another back room and heard Shelby yell the warning,

"I looked to see what was wrong and stuck around to see if there was anything I could do and then snuck out," Dennis said.

The first alarm was sounded at 12:25 p.m., with the next two alarms coming at 12:28 and 12:45. In all, 15 engines, four ladder trucks and a special unit were called. Fire Chief Louis Rozsa said approximately 100 men, including 23 who were off duty, helped fight the blaze.

At 2:45 p.m., Rozsa declared the fire under control and ordered some of the equipment returned to stations.

The firm employs 19 people. Between 12 and 18 persons were inside the building when the fire began.

All of the employees escaped from the structure safely, among them Nancy Barlow, 25; Shirley Taylor, 29; Thelma Shrout, 34, and her sister-in-law, Helen Shrout, 35.

"When I got here I saw mostly smoke," said District Chief Howard Grothjan, who arrived at the scene first and took charge of the equipment.

There were some flames on the first and second floors, but they hadn't spread into the third and fourth floors, he said.

At 1:30 p.m., flames shot through the roof of the building, rising like a giant smokestack, as the fire methodically burned its way through the structure.

Less than five minutes later the south half of the east wall caved in, and firemen on a ladder truck parked nearby scurried to escape flying bricks.

The north part of that wall collapsed at 2:08 p.m., but the other walls continued to stand.

"It's coming down," Grothjan yelled. And the half wall folded slowly in front of gigantic flames, spraying brick onto a small, leafless tree. A fire extension ladder that resembled a mechanical giraffe spit a thin stream of water into mustard-colored smoke.

A few minutes later, Robert Robbeloth, 66, a retired district chief who had been watching the blaze in front of the building, suffered a stroke and was taken to Miami Valley Hospital. He was listed in poor condition there.

More than 20 city policemen were called and Box 21 also assisted.

Shortly before 3 p.m., an emergency unit from the Dayton Power and Light Company cut off power at a pole located just south of the building.

Approximately 20 telephones were put out of service, and telephone cable splicers could not re-route the lines, because of the danger of the south wall collapsing.

Rozsa said his men will remain on the scene until at least tomorrow, to make sure the burlap and other material are completely free of flame.

Note: As competing reporters began to arrive and I was concluding my interviews, I asked Wagner, the fellow who first spotted the fire, if he liked beer.

"Yeah," he said with a grin.

I took a 10-dollar bill from my wallet — which bought a lot of suds back then — and said, "Why don't you guys go have a few brews."

Wagner grinned as he accepted the money. I think he knew what was going through my mind. He and the others began walking away, presumably toward their cars, as the inferno raged on.

When I submitted my monthly expense account, Bill Bennington, an assistant city editor, asked me about the $10 I listed for beer while covering the fire. Everybody knew that I was a teetotaler. After I explained the expenditure, he broke into laughter — and approved payment. The *Journal Herald* had exclusively carried the best eyewitness accounts.

He Seeks Trouble, Usually Finds It

Dayton *Journal Herald*, Jan. 27, 1966

It was a simple assignment, one that, I'm sure, had been made before at several newspapers: Ride with a police officer for an entire shift some night. But it turned out to be one of the most fascinating experiences I had as a reporter.

Each working day, Ernie Fleming gets into an automobile, drives around the city of Dayton for six to eight hours and looks for trouble.

And he finds it.

It may develop at any time, depending on which shift Fleming may be working — the one that starts at 8 in the morning, or the relief that begins with mushrooming traffic at 4 in the afternoon, or the midnight trick.

Despite the inconvenience of ever-changing hours, and despite the danger inherent in looking for trouble — Ernie Fleming likes being a policeman.

The 28-year-old Fleming may not be the typical police officer, and yet, he's not unique either.

He knows how it feels to be called "cop," and he winces at what he feels is a general loss of respect for policemen. He feels the pay should be higher. His varying hours disrupt his family life.

Still, Ernie Fleming is happy in what he is doing, because for him there are powerful, intangible rewards in being a law enforcement officer.

"I don't like to see other people abused or taken advantage of," he says.

He talked easily the other afternoon while he ate his big meal for the day at 2 p.m., two hours before he was to go on duty as one of four "selective patrol" units.

"I mean, you know, I said to myself, you were here for a purpose, what are you going to do," he continued.

The lean, 5-foot-11, 160-pounder said it was in the Navy, while he was doing shore patrol duty, that he decided police work would be best for him.

"Some people know cars, some people know airplanes, I know people. And I think that's the reason I decided to be a policeman, because policemen work with people."

He got up from his chair, ran a hand over his brown crew cut, and got the milk container from the refrigerator.

Returning, he scooped up a portion of tuna casserole, prepared by his wife, the former Mary Mullins. He poured milk for four-year-old Sheri, told two-year-old Karen to sit still.

"The hero is the guy who works at Delco, say, who comes home to his family and doesn't bother anyone. He just goes about his business. I'll help protect that guy. I hate parasites and young punks who pick on elderly people."

Fleming admits, however, there are times when his morale drops.

To get inspired again, he will usually go to the basement of his home — a bungalow-style structure in Cornell Heights for which he is paying $11,500 — and read from a page torn from a magazine.

The page sits atop a low filing cabinet. The words are those of an American president, but not one of the more often quoted chief executives, such as Franklin D. Roosevelt or John F. Kennedy.

Instead, the words of Calvin Coolidge inspire Fleming.

"To join in this high enterprise (police work) means the surrender of much individual freedom ...," said Coolidge, then governor of Massachusetts, during the Boston police strike of 1919.

Fleming has read these Coolidge words over and over:

" ... When the law fails, barbarianism flourishes. Whoever flouts the law, whoever brings it into disrespect, whoever connives at its evasion is an enemy of civilization. Change it as you will, but observe it always, that is government..."

Fleming feels strongly about that paragraph, and he says, "We need professionals to do the job."

He left the table to get into his uniform, asked Mary if she would give his badge a quick shine. A few moments later he emerged, putting on his leather jacket and service revolver last.

"The gun? Well, it's just part of the job. You hope you don't have to use it, but you can't be afraid not to."

Fleming arrived at the Safety building a little early, joked around with fellow officers and then stepped into the assembly room for roll call and to pick up the day's information on stolen cars, burglaries and other crimes.

Then, shortly after 4 p.m., he got into his cruiser. "Selective patrol," he explained, "is a new phase of law enforcement in Dayton.

"We're told, more or less: find the trouble and stop it in your own manner. I think this is good. A man should be given the right to use his own judgment."

He started driving to his assigned area for the night, the West Side.

At Germantown and Williams streets, he watched a Negro man help a white woman start her car. Fleming stopped the man, Otis Fountain, 45, of 63 South Plaza Avenue, and thanked him.

"People, something about them. You know what makes this job worth it? One morning, about 2 o'clock, I'm checking doors on Fifth Street and this Negro businessman stops me and thanks me.

"There's too much trouble out here,' he says. 'Muggings and burglaries.' As I started to walk off, he said, 'Officer, God bless you.' That chokes you up. Well, anyway, it did me."

At 5:17 p.m., he turned down an alley off Germantown. "Oh, hell yes, I get scared. Fear keeps you going. Fear keeps you sharp; you have to sense things. If you weren't afraid, you would walk right into something blind."

Darkness fell over the city. Outside it was cold and the activity relatively light.

Fleming drove to St. Elizabeth Hospital's emergency ward, to check activity there, make out a couple of reports and get a cup of coffee.

Cal Warner, working a regular patrol on the West Side, arrived a few minutes later, joined Ernie and began to discuss the current salary proposals.

"Pay's the big factor with me," said Warner, who has been on the force about the same amount of time as Fleming, six years.

"I'm optimistic about Hall (new Mayor Dave Hall)," Ernie said. "Crawford (City Commissioner Don Crawford), I think, is on our side. He seems to understand our problems."

Back in the car, Fleming talked about police professionalism. "We need more men like Parker in Los Angeles (Chief William Parker) and J. Edgar Hoover, that kind of professionalism. Then we'll get our due recognition.

"Yes, being called a cop bothers you. You can't help it. You try not to show it and grin and take it in stride, but it's there. I don't know why.

"Just about everybody I deal with makes more money than I do. That's one thing. You feel one cut underneath them. I don't know, it's just the accepted level, I guess, but it bothers me. It has to."

At 10 p.m., a report of a personal injury accident was broadcast.

"They called for an ambulance awfully fast." Fleming decided to assist, though he was 15 minutes away.

When he arrived, he learned that traffic needed to be directed at Cincinnati Street and Nicholas Road. He went to that point, set up flares.

He had routed more than a hundred cars off of Nicholas Road, going west, onto Cincinnati Street when he had a narrow brush with death. That was at 10:52 p.m.

As Fleming stood in a little island area, to the right of the inside lane, a car with a woman behind the wheel bore down on him, ignored his signal, and sped through the road block, barely missing both the cruiser and him.

Fleming whirled, caught the license number and then radioed ahead, where the accident was being investigated, and told the officers to send the woman back.

"I think you merit a citation, don't you?" Fleming said to the woman after she had returned.

"I wish you wouldn't give me a ticket, I'm late already," she replied.

Fleming walked back to the cruiser to write out a citation.

"I'm a divorcee trying to support my daughter and that officer is really going to mess me up at work," the woman complained to a bystander.

After more than an hour of directing traffic in the bitter cold, Fleming went to St. Elizabeth Hospital again, to make out some final reports and warm up with coffee.

At 11:42 p.m., he took a last swig from his cup. "Not much of a night," he said, getting up from the chair.

Shortly before midnight, he checked into the safety building and walked to where he had parked his 1961 Karmen Ghia — the one he recently bought and is making payments on.

He would drive home, he said, have a snack with Mary and then go to his basement, where he would study for the next sergeant examination.

And maybe, too, some time before going upstairs to bed, Ernie Fleming might reach over to that low, sea green filing cabinet and read again Cal Coolidge's words about policemen and the law.

A Journalist's Journey

Ever Want To Join Circus? JH Reporter Did For Day

Dayton *Journal Herald,* March 25, 1966

Tony Svet, the assistant city editor I mentioned earlier, approached my desk one day shortly after I reported for work at 2 p.m. "Now, don't take this the wrong way," he said, "but we'd like you to be a clown at the circus and write a first-person piece."

I smiled. "Great idea," I said.

Svet smiled back and said, "Doty will meet you at the fairgrounds," meaning chief photographer Bob Doty.

My story ran with four photos on the local news section page the next day. A Page 1 "tickler" photo of me about to kiss a woman on the cheek also ran.

There were myriad days when I loved being a journalist. That day was one of them.

Tiny tots with dancing eyes—their mommies' and daddies' dancing too — and cotton candy and greasepaint and animals — and clowns.

I was a part of it all yesterday afternoon, even to the point of being called "Mosco the Clown."

Behind the facade of a ludicrous face — red nose, and all — and a bear-fur coat that swam on my five-foot frame, I joined six other clowns for the opening of the Shrine circus, the 24th annual Antioch Temple extravaganza.

Youngsters, some bewildered, some old hands, began to march into the Fairgrounds Coliseum shortly after 3:30 p.m., and backstage I was being converted into a clown by a veteran of the business.

His name was Harold Simmons, from Australia, and he stood a foot shorter than me.

"Damn bloody 'ard to make up someone else," he said, applying greasepaint and white powder.

The final touch was a battered brown derby, which sat snugly on my head while my arms and hands became lost somewhere in the heavy fur coat.

I walked without assurance, as if in never-never land, toward the grandstand, and an elderly woman tugged at her grandchild and said, "See, Bobby, see the clown!"

Suddenly I was no longer Ray Moscowitz, general assignment reporter. He was now a man of the past.

"Hi, Bobby," I said in a funny little voice. "I'm Mosco the Clown."

And I believed it.

And suddenly again I felt a tingle of joy shoot through me, because while a newspaperman — often called cynical — was behind that greasepaint, on the surface was a funny, happy man who possessed a unique power to explode laughter.

And in front of him were happy people.

Some of the kiddies were afraid to shake my hand or sit on my lap, and they cuddled close to Mommy. But for the most part, their eyes stared in awe, and their popcorn was forgotten and their world was now me.

And I loved it, and I found myself bounding around the coliseum like a kid in a candy store, not knowing what crazy antics to perform next, not knowing where to stop next, not knowing where to extract my own joy by oozing joy.

Vietnam? NATO? Never heard of them.

Finally, the actual show was about to unfold, and Gene Randow, the top-billed clown, and Simmons moved under the make-believe Big Top to warm up the fast-filling house.

Now the acts began ... the Four Kelroys and Welde's Bears, and the Shrine band, under the direction of Paul Blagg, matched the atmosphere to perfection.

I went downstairs to the dressing quarters.

"When do we go on?" I asked for the fifth or sixth time. And when someone said after Stebbing's Boxer Dogs — a great act, incidentally

— I said, "Yeah, I see the schedule here, and I felt somehow like a veteran after my initial 30-minute stint.

And then the boxers ran off and the spotlight blazed front and center — and for the first time, my heart went thumpity-thump-thump.

We ran — Hal Simmons, Rocko, Larry Benner, L'il Jimmy Armstrong and Frenchie — behind Randow, shouting and acting nuttier than peanut brittle.

Oh, it was fun, and I was not aware of a thousand eyes being out there — only people, people like me, laughing and eating and drinking ... and then the firecracker Randow lighted boomed out, and I ran like a frightened idiot ... and then suddenly it was over ...

"You're silly!" a little girl shouted, and I shouted back, "You're a thilly-dilly, too," and I poked out my tongue.

Now I was downstairs again, and as I scrubbed the makeup from my face, I asked Randow how long he had been a clown.

"Third generation. My father died backstage one night as he was taking off his makeup. Clowning is all I know — and if there were no circuses, I don't know what I'd do — but then if there was no circuses, what would kids do?"

I chatted a few minutes with the six men who had been my fellow clowns — then left them talking about the circus.

Outside, a cold blast of the final vestiges of winter hit me, blowing away the last of my façade — and the tiny tots and the animals and cotton candy were no more.

And I thought, as a seal barked in the distance, God bless the world for little boys and girls and circuses and clowns — and in that order.

London Action Moves Along Kings Road

Dayton *Journal Herald*, July 21, 1967

In 1967, I asked the *Journal Herald* for a six-week leave of absence to tour Europe. The JH not only granted it, but offered to pay me to write a series of articles on European life. The reporting experience was extremely valuable, and the money I received helped finance my trip. Here's the editor's note that the JH ran before each of the 14 articles I wrote.

(EDITOR'S NOTE: Raymond Moscowitz, Journal Herald copy editor, is touring Europe this summer. This is another in a series of articles he will write on European life as he finds it.)

LONDON — Hippies making the India scene, marijuana, young debs dressed in ruffles and lace, psychedelic music, a turned-on frivolity racing through the pubs — this is Kings Road.

It is London's latest "in" — a two-and-a-half mile sliver of fashion houses, restaurants, shops, pubs and markets in the chic Chelsea section.

The four-year reign of Carnaby Street, which relied solely on mod clothes to attract the "in crowd," died about six months ago, people on the street agree — and so now it's The World's End and Chelsea Potter for brew and Sidney Smith's and Dandy Fashions for clothes.

The in crowd is an odd mixture consisting of young swingers with respectable jobs, do-nothings, pot-smoking hippies and the young, rich in royalty debutantes. Such a kind of combination frequenting one area points up the current disintegration of class in England.

Dave Newble, a 21-year-old paint salesman from Crawley, an "overspill" town of 100,000 30 miles south of London, sat opposite an NCR cash register at the Potter bar and described Carnaby Street as "sort of a one-night affair" compared with Kings Road.

At Sidney Smith's, one of the 30 clothing establishments crammed along the two-and-a-half miles, Monty Barak said essentially the same thing, asserting that "people got fed up with Carnaby because it's all the same."

Barak, 24, a salesman in the store, and David Millman, 27, another salesman, talked of Kings Road as an area where cocktail affairs have been replaced by "kinky" (way out) parties featuring love-ins, where the drug scene is prominent — from hippies to the debs — and where the latest fashion trends are set, and where, as Millman called it, a "transformation of the sexes in taking place — unfortunately."

LSD? It's just starting to make its way onto the scene, Millman said, and it will give Kings Road extra impetus.

The long hair and the Beatles came before Kings Road's "time," but Barak noted that "long hair was here before God."

The Beatles have scored with the Kings Road crowd, says Mick Burke, a 19-year-old salesman at Strickland's Record shop, but, he notes, psychedelic music — free form, loud guitars and organs, electrical gimmicks — is big, too.

Fashion-wise, there are differences. Aside from their extremely long hair and pathetic appearance, the hippies can be spotted by beads and bells hanging from their clothes, possibly from a shaggy belt holding up plain, bell bottom white trousers, or a dirt-splotched miniskirt.

Meanwhile, the rich young debs — Millman referred to them as "the honorables" — rely on the Dandy Shop, where they buy clothes from the Regency period — ruffled and lace shirts and blouses, items made of velvet.

Mixed in between are young swingers who still prefer the wide, flat paisley ties and paisley shirts. But, Millman says, the preferences are American Levi pants, made of corduroy and available in an assortment of colors from beige to maroon.

Chelsea Potter, the World's End and Colville — the latter is headquarters for the gay set — are the most popular of about 10 pubs, but no one, including the people who go to these places, seems to know exactly why.

Derek Asprill, 34, an electrical engineer from Crawley, sipped some warm ale as he brewed a thought and then said: "Everybody goes there (to the in pubs) because somebody goes there first."

A 26-year-old writer from Liverpool, Lyle Jones, came up with the bromidic "it's where the action is, I guess."

Newble said he felt it was simply a "happy atmosphere" at Potter's which attracted people, as formality — and old ways — are brushed aside by an ale-sogged bar, cheese and crackers, sandwiches and sausages.

And then he said — out of nowhere — "You know, you Americans ought to get out of Vietnam."

Night Callers

Dayton *Journal Herald*, Nov. 6, 1968

This is a column I wrote for the editorial page after a slice-of-life newspaper experience that is still fresh in my mind.

He came up from behind me as I leaned back in the chair against the little partition that separates the lobby from the city room and said "Hey."

Friday night. Eleven twenty-seven. Thirty-three minutes before deadline. No sweat. Copy cleared.

"Are you sober?" I asked."

"Sure," he said. "I want to talk to the editor."

"Well, I'm afraid he's not here right now," I half-smiled, preparing myself for what appeared to be the "character of the week."

They never stop coming in this business. They might come in person — alcohol-trapped — or call you on the phone, usually alcohol-trapped.

"Okay, then," he said — and now I could smell the brew — "let me talk to the next highest guy in charge."

"That's me," I said, matter-of-factly — and I thought about the guy who once called wanting to know if goats had veins.

"Who're you?" he wanted to know.

"I'm the night city editor," I said.

"I've been robbed and the cops ain't going to do a damn thing about it." He pulled up a chair, lighted a cigarette.

I thought about the man who once called shortly before 1 a.m. and wanted to know how high the Empire State building is — in-feet and without the tower. Twelve hundred fifty.

"See, I'm walking out of this bar on West Third and this guy grabs my money, 97 bucks, all I got on me," he says.

Then there was the time a woman called and wanted to know who was worth more, Johnny Mathis or Floyd Patterson.

"So I go to the cops," he continued, "and give them this license number and they tell me they can't do a damn thing until Monday."

I remembered, now, the time a guy came off the elevator, close to midnight, clean shaven and well dressed — and just cried for about a minute and didn't say anything. And then just left.

"Well," I said, "I'm sure the police are trying to find the guy." I was still matter-of-fact.

"Naw, they ain't, and I want them to hound this guy like they hounded me," he said.

"Married?"

"Yeah, two kids, 22 years and I ain't got no beef."

"Got a job?"

"Yeah," he said. A window washer.

"Well, I'm sure the police are doing something for you," I said, now trying to dismiss him.

"Listen, I did 11 years for manslaughter and armed robbery — oh, it was legit — and they hounded me, see, and now I want them to hound this guy," he said.

I took his name, picked up the phone and called the desk sergeant — a guy named Prugh — and told him the guy's story, and Prugh assured me they were looking for the guy who had made the hit and that the Monday-morning bit meant only that the man was supposed to come to the detective section and tell the police just what had happened.

"That's bull-can-I-use-your-phone?"

Sure.

"Hello, Paul?"

He was calling his boss. He'd walked the straight and narrow — that's the expression he used — for more than 10 years now, washing windows, and now he didn't want to be the victim of a raw deal.

"Paul, I been robbed . . . I'm at the *Journal Herald*, Paul, and they ain't got no sympathy for me. Remember, Pauley, how they got me?"

I got a little peeved. I had sympathy for the man. I signaled Dave Zimmerman, the copy boy, and asked to see if we had anything in the library on him.

Now he was off the phone — and he was getting madder, but not louder.

Dave came back from the library and handed me an envelope. It told of the robbery, and yes, what the guy had told me was true, he'd been a two-time loser in Ohio.

I got a little interested. "Listen," I said, "don't go out and futz around and get yourself in a jam."

"Naw, I'm gonna find that guy like they hounded me, 'cause I paid and hell ..."

Was he hungry?

"Yeah, but I'm OK, but what about the kids next week?"

"Look," I said, "let me give you a buck and you can run over to the White Tower and grab a burger and a cup of coffee."

"Man, I don't take charity," he said.

Yes, he was proud, I could see, and I said, "Look, don't go out and do something rash. Here, take a buck and get yourself something to eat and just cool off."

No, he reiterated, he didn't go for charity.

I stressed to him it wasn't charity, but no, he wasn't taking any dollar from me.

"Be thankful you're alive and you have a wife that's stood by you for 22 years and just chalk this off as a bad experience," I said, suddenly a little embarrassed.

There was some hesitation now, and he looked at me hard, and then he got up and stuck out his hand. We shook.

"You know, you're OK," he said. "You're right. Hell, we'll make out next week, we'll be all right" — and then he was gone.

An hour later I went home, had a bowl of cream of mushroom soup (in wine sauce) and wondered who was worth more, Johnny Mathis or Floyd Patterson.

Love Nibbles at Dwindling Lithuanian Clan

Dayton Journal Herald, Jan. 15, 1969

I was assigned to write a series of articles on the largest ethnic groups that lived in Dayton. After the series of 10 articles ran, the Dayton school system asked the *Journal Herald* to package several thousand copies for use as part of the schools' history curriculum. I didn't think much of that at the time, but over the years, it brought great satisfaction to me.

Shaped like a slice of pie, "Little Texas" consumes much of North Dayton and continues to be the population center for the city's Lithuanian community.

Like other immigrants who settled in North Dayton, the Lithuanians arrived with Texas-style pride — and thus the large neighborhood bounded by Leo Street on the north, Valley Street on the south and the Miami-Mad rivers apex to the west acquired the "Little Texas" label.

In 1902, the Lithuanian community numbered 300. Growth since then has leveled off at 200 families. But the pride the immigrants brought with them has not.

Frank Ambrose, 29, of 47 Brandt Street, says he's proud of his Lithuanian background simply because "it's different." A supervisor at Dayton Tire and Rubber Company, Ambrose says he enjoys someone asking, "Where the hell is Lithuania?"

Ambrose's sister, Mrs. Elinor Sluzas, 40, of 55 Brandt Street, says she's proud "because we all look for something extra special in ourselves. In our case, we have the oldest living language in the world."

Religious worship is also something special for Lithuanians, who are overwhelmingly Catholic.

Lithuania is called the "Land of Crosses," notes Mrs. John Scott, 51, of 1907 Leo Street, because of the many roadside shrines and crosses that can be seen throughout the nation.

Mrs. Scott, who has a small Lithuanian shrine in her backyard, explained that the people had to walk for miles to church and the crosses marked places where churchgoers could rest and pray on the way.

In 1911, Cincinnati Archbishop Henry Moeller gave the Lithuanians here permission to organize a parish and they proceeded to build a church on 1.1 acres of land at the southwest corner of Leo and Lukaswitz (now Rita) streets.

That southwest corner remains the hub around which the Lithuanians, who describe themselves as "very clannish," revolve.

Lionginas (Louie) Prasmantas, 40, of 1023 Dodgson Court, drifted into the North Dayton clan when he visited here 19 years ago as a displaced person who had come to Ohio under the sponsorship of a Millersburg farmer.

Now a U.S. citizen, Prasmantas was attracted to Dayton by a Lithuanian picnic. He liked what he saw and is now involved as a postal worker.

Picnics and other festive occasions are commonplace among the Lithuanians. Among the special dates is the commemoration of independence from the Russians on Feb. 16, 1918.

Festive occasions — like St. Caslmir patron saint's day on March 4 (Lithuanians "share" the saint with Poles) — call for lots of foods. And when it comes to food, the generally big-boned Lithuanians go for meat and potatoes.

"Don't forget to mention kugelis," says Ambrose, who stands 6-4 and weighs 235 pounds.

Kugelis is a potato dish in which potatoes are grated with onion and fried bits of bacon or ham and then beaten into half a dozen eggs and cream. After seasoning, it's baked in a casserole until golden brown, sliced and served with sour cream.

The leveling off of the Lithuanian community has resulted from an increase in mixed marriages. The Lithuanians have a problem frequent among ethnic groups here — there are not enough of them to allow young people to find their kind of marriage partner among those with the same background.

"Arrangements" are sometimes tried here, says Mrs. Scott, because, like the Poles, the Lithuanians strongly discourage mixed marriage.

"But getting a Lithuanian boy and girl together — you just can't hardly do it," she says.

"Those with money still try hard, though," adds Mrs. Sluzas, explaining that sometimes an affluent Lithuanian will send his son or daughter to another city to meet someone.

Others work through the Knights of Lithuania to obtain a mate.

The Knights of Lithuania is a nationwide, coed organization whose motto is "For God and Country" as it strives to free Lithuania from Soviet domination, according to Stanley Vaitkus of 518 Hialeah Court, Vandalia. Vaitkus, national vice president of the organization, said the local chapter, Council 96, has about 100 members.

It was through the organization that Vaitkus found his wife, becoming engaged to a girl from Providence, R.I., at the New York wedding of Daytonian Mike Petkus, 45, of 260 Air Street, "Little Texas." Petkus had gone to Gotham to marry a New York City girl.

Vaitkus is a manufacturer's representative, while Petkus delivers mail.

Frank Ambrose, the tire worker, classifies himself and the others who live in North Dayton as members of a "comfortable middle class."

For the most part, the Lithuanians remain employed in the industrial force, but Ambrose and others are quick to stress that, unlike those who first came to Dayton, they have moved into skilled labor positions.

"Our parents wanted something better for us," said Louie Prasmantas' wife, Catherine. "They wanted us to get more education than they received."

Professionally, there are four Lithuanian doctors, noted Rita Ambrose, who shares the house at 47 Brandt Street with her brother

Frank.

Another Lithuanian who considers himself a professional is Stanley Kavy, a Dayton police sergeant referred to by many Lithuanians as the "mayor" of North Dayton.

Kavy, who is quick to note that fellow policemen Capt. John Belskis and Sgt. Stanley Burneka are Lithuanians, says he got the honorary title during his college days at Ohio State when the older people, who couldn't speak very much English, came to him with their problems and interpretations of life in their new land.

Nolan, Zipperian contracts deny Kays 2 appointments

Frankfort *Times*, Dec. 1, 1971

As an editor in the grassroots, I made it a point to get out of the newsroom at least twice a week for an hour or so to see what was going on in town. My visits with key people usually resulted in stories that I either assigned or wrote.

Two department-head appointments normally made by the mayor have been denied Mayor-elect Clifford G. Kays because of contractual agreements, the *Times* learned today.

Kays confirmed contracts were signed Friday, Sept. 24, at a special Board of Works meeting by Charles H. "Red" Nolan, City Light and Power Plant superintendent, and Richard E. Zipperian, Frankfort Water Works superintendent.

The contracts were offered by the present Board of Works composed of Mayor James Brown, City Engineer Blair Allen and City Attorney Gene Robbins.

Robbins, Kays, Zipperian, Nolan and Clerk-Treasurer Mary Jane McMahon all said that, to their knowledge, this is the first time such contracts have been offered by the city. Robbins, Nolan and Zipperian added that the contracts are not unusual.

Mrs. McMahon said she could not comment on the contracts, except to say that she signed them, by law, because her signature is needed to verify the signature of Mayor Brown.

"I don't know about the special meeting," Mrs. McMahon said, "but I have a copy of the minutes for it."

Robbins said he took the minutes himself, because Mrs. McMahon was not available for the meeting.

Robbins, who has been appointed by Kays to continue in his post, said contracts were not presented at the board's weekly meeting on Wednesday, Sept. 22, "because they weren't ready at that time."

Asked why the contracts were not presented at the board's next regular Wednesday meeting — instead of a special meeting which does not require any kind of legal notice — Robbins said: "I'm not sure. I suppose we wanted to get them out of the way as soon as possible. We had been discussing the contracts for a long time.

"I told the mayor on Thursday (Sept. 23) that the contracts were ready and said, 'Whenever you're ready to get together, it's OK.' We decided to meet on Friday."

Asked why there was no announcement regarding the contracts after they were signed, Robbins said: "I don't know. Sometimes there are announcements on those things and sometimes there aren't."

The contracts call for Nolan and Zipperian to retain their positions until Dec. 31, 1973.

Nolan's monthly salary under the contract is for $1,223.84, while Zipperian's pact calls for $889.33 a month.

The contracts also allow the board "at its discretion and subject to the provisions of applicable law" to increase — but not decrease — the salaries.

Nolan or Zipperian may be removed from their jobs, according to their contracts, "for cause," after written notice and a hearing by the Board of Works.

Asked to define "for cause," Robbins replied: "It depends. It could be something involving stealing or being drunk on the job. It could also mean incompetence; this would be a matter of judgment. This would require a board hearing."

Kays, whose Democratic administration takes office Jan. 1, said this morning he first heard of the contracts the night of the election, after he had been declared the winner.

"My first reaction was surprise, of course," Kays said. "At that time, I did not have any individuals in mind for those jobs. Consequently, I have not given those two appointments thought, because of the contracts."

Kays said his first move was to determine if the contracts were valid, and Robbins advised him that they were.

"I feel bound by the contracts as long as they are legal," Kays said, "but I intend to get a legal opinion from the state attorney general's office."

Kays continued: "However, I assume I will begin my administration with Mr. Nolan and Mr. Zipperian in their respective jobs until some kind of legal decision is made. I fully intend to work with these men on the basis that we're part of a team dedicated to making Frankfort a better place to live in."

Asked what action he would take if the contracts proved to be invalid, Kays said: "I'll have to consider that after the decision. I simply can't say at this point."

Kays thus far has appointed, along with Robbins, James Marcum as head of the street department and Frank Hemmerling police chief.

Robbins admitted that while the Board of Works agreed to have the contracts offered to Nolan and Zipperian, he was the catalyst.

Robbins said he pushed the idea, "because I felt the contracts would be an advantage to the city. We're dealing with two continuing technical positions. It seems to me, the city wouldn't want superintendents who would be looking for jobs before a new administration came in, before that new administration could see what kind of job those people are doing."

The attorney asserted "a new administration doesn't have the experience to make decisions of this sort." He added: "There are certain jobs you can do contracts on. The statutes allow contracts to be awarded in some jobs, and technically, the Board of Works hires utility people on the mayor's recommendation. But you can't go around giving contracts to all appointed people. I don't think you would want contracts for the police chief and the street commissioner, for example.

"But jobs that are highly technical in nature need a certain caliber of people. It could be a great disadvantage if a new administration had to make a change."

Robbins pointed out that Kays could make a change after two

years.

Asked to comment on the contracts, Nolan and Zipperian pointed out that such agreements are signed in other cities.

"It's not uncommon in the utility field," Zipperian said, noting that many communities in Southern Indiana, "around the Columbus area," have such contracts.

Nolan said that while "it has not been a practice" here, his contract is not unusual. He said contracts have become standard practice in recent years, adding that Logansport and Peru are two communities he knows of with such agreements.

Nolan was originally appointed by former Democrat mayor Robert Kirkwood and retained by present Republican Mayor James Brown. Zipperian, who has worked with the water works for 15 years, was appointed by Brown.

GOP blood flows in Clinton County

Frankfort *Times*, April 1, 1972

Politics in Clinton County, Ind., was like a blood sport during my six-year stint as managing editor of the newspaper. This analysis, which required some tough reporting, is an example.

Some say it began two years ago, others say it was four. It doesn't make any difference today. The blood is following in the Clinton County Republican Party.

There is constant fighting within any party — such as a minor feud these days among the Democrats over endorsement of a gubernatorial candidate — but the GOP battle here has taken on fratricidal proportions.

Those in the know are hesitant to talk for the record, but it's no secret among party regulars that essentially the party is split into two camps, with County Chairman Ralph Hinshaw heading one and Lucille Wooffendale, his colorful vice chairman, leading the other. But, like they say at the ballpark, you need a scorecard to figure out who's who in the contest. And even then, the picture gets fuzzy.

After James Brown's election as mayor in 1967, the Republicans, a close-knit group, found themselves solidly in control of City Hall and the Courthouse.

Then the squabbling began.

When Brown appointed Gene Robbins, a Democrat lawyer, as city attorney, it infuriated Republican lawyer James T. "Tom" Robison. Robison held the post for the first year of Brown's administration, but his election as State Representative forced him to step down. He assumed another Republican lawyer would be offered the job.

But Brown went with Robbins, who had formerly served as city attorney, reportedly on the recommendation of GOP Clerk-Treasurer Mary Jane McMahon. The first major wound was opened.

The shifting sands of dissension continued until May of 1970, when the newly-elected precinct committeemen met on Saturday after the Tuesday primary to choose a County Chairman.

Noble Hodgen, whose record as chairman over the years was decidedly successful, walked into the meeting and said he was through. Though Hodgen's resignation had been rumored, the actual move of stepping down took many by surprise.

Hodgen then allegedly forced the election of Hinshaw, making him his own hand-picked man. Robison, a 20-year committeeman, admits that he walked out of the session, angered about the way the meeting was drifting.

Robison stayed long enough to nominate Mrs. Wooffendale as vice chairman and see her elected. But shortly later, he was asked to be treasurer, said no and stalked out.

"I wanted a committeeman to be chairman," Robison says when asked about the meeting. "Ralph had no experience as a committeeman. He never worked in the vineyards. He was always out selling the wine."

Robison has long sided with Mrs. Wooffendale, who has been vice chairman for 17 years and has a political track record that would make anyone envious.

A seasoned political pro, Mrs. Wooffendale eats, sleeps and breathes politics. After serving as County Clerk for eight years she is now seeking Robison's seat in the legislature. He announced in December he was through with the General Assembly, because it was taking too much of his time.

Does Robison seek Hinshaw's post? Robison answers: "Yes, I'm very interested if the situation looks favorable." He continues: "We've had one central committee meeting since Ralph was elected. It was during the city election, and I'm not sure what went on at that session."

There is no question that Hinshaw will seek re-election. "I'll run in May, and it looks good for me," he says vehemently. "There are a number of people who have called and urged me to run again."

When asked, Hinshaw says there is no major split in the party, but he doesn't say it very forcefully. Eventually, a tinge of bitterness comes through and he speaks boldly — at times saying, "This is off the record."

What is on the record is this:

"A few individuals have run this party as a virtual dictatorship for the last six or eight years. This is obvious. As chairman I've tried to give the party back to the people.

"In October of 1970, right after I had been elected, Tom and Lucille started a rumor that I was going to be dumped. They'll deny it, of course. But I have friends, too, you know."

Meanwhile, Mrs. Wooffendale is in a three-way primary fight with two political newcomers, David Tudor of Westfield and Rossville attorney Richard Langston.

Understandably, she is reluctant to comment on the wide open gash in the party, but there is no question that she is upset with Hinshaw and vice versa. She blames the party's solid trouncing in the last city election, in which Roy Ayers lost the mayoral race to Cliff Kays by 67 votes, squarely on the shoulders of Hinshaw and Mrs. McMahon, who at one time was a Wooffendale protégé in the county clerk's office before moving into her present city post.

Hinshaw's view of the city election debacle is considerably different:

"The city judge race cost us the election. Roger Miller (then the incumbent) said he would run again, but at the last minute, he said the Robisons (for whom he worked and is now a full partner) would not let him.

"Lu came to me at the last minute to get somebody. I had had Steve Bock (of then Ryan and Hartzel) all set, but he said he wouldn't run if Roger did. When I went to Steve at the last minute, he said no, it was too late.

"If Steve had run, we'd have had a strong judge candidate, which would have given us the overall strength that we needed to win. The judge race is what beat us."

Under Hodgen's regime, Republican unity was about as solid as possible. He and Mrs. Wooffendale were — and still are — organization pros who knew how to get out the party faithful, assuring GOP victories from school boards to State Representative.

But a look at precinct races and delegate battles for this May clearly shows that the old unity is gone. Former Mayor Brown, allegedly Hinshaw's man, is taking on Sheriff Robert Kelley for a precinct post. And in another tussle, Mrs. Wooffendale's sister, Mrs. Betty Miller, is pitted against former County Prosecutor Carol Grafton, who also has learned much about the political process through the years from Mrs. Wooffendale.

Hinshaw admits he got Brown to run against the sheriff. "They do it me, I'll do it to them," he says bluntly.

Like Mrs. Wooffendale, Grafton cannot afford to get involved openly in the blood-letting. He has the job of coordinating local Republicans who support Dr. Otis Bowen for the GOP gubernatorial nomination, and thus needs all the friends he has.

So the whispers and phone calls and notes are making the rounds — some hot enough to make a king-sized elephant jump with all four feet off the ground.

Whether the Republicans can somehow patch their many wounds in time before the fall election is doubtful.

But at the same time, whether the Democrats here can take advantage of the split is an unknown factor, at best.

Grassroots politics in Clinton County, always a fascinating animal to watch, promises to offer even more fun and games this major election year.

De facto secrecy

Frankfort *Times*, June 5, 1972

Like most editors, I fought government secrecy throughout my career — to the point that in December 1998 the Hoosier State Press Association established the "Ray Moscowitz Award" to honor newspapers that go beyond the call of duty to fight secrecy. (The HSPA could have just as easily named the award after several other editors.)

This is one of my early editorials or columns that dealt with hindering the public's right to know.

This year's negotiations between the Frankfort School Board and the Classroom Teachers Association point out something that has been practiced here for years.

We call it de facto secrecy.

In actuality, the school board, whether it is dealing with bus chassis bids or teachers' salaries, probably acts within the law.

That is to say, the board takes no official action, such as voting to award contracts on anything ranging from gasoline to frying oil, in an executive session.

But for all intents and purposes, many of the more controversial matters the board deals with are handled in secrecy.

Here's how:

The board opens its meeting at 7:30 or 8 p.m. It drags along until, say, 10:30, dispensing with routine matters. Then, the board goes into an executive session, to discuss personnel, which is entirely legitimate and expected. Finally, near midnight, the board comes out of executive session and declares the meeting open again.

Such procedure is the rule — not the exception — with the Frankfort board. At its last meeting, the board came out of the executive session at 12:45 a.m. and did not finish its regular meeting until almost 2 o'clock in the morning.

What all of this amounts to is this: The board discourages the average citizen from attending its meeting. Deliberately or not, the board often forces the average person, who probably is due at work at 8 o'clock the next day, to hang on until the wee hours of the morning before crucial matters are brought to the floor.

We think that public meetings should not be allowed to continue past 11 p.m., if at all possible. Certainly, governmental organizations should not still be meeting at 1:30 in the morning.

There are some board members who have pressed for more open and better-planned meetings. But they are in the minority.

So, while Indiana's Public Disclosure Law (Burns 57-601, 57-606) is probably not being broken, the confidence and support of local taxpayers are being undermined by this practice.

The *Times* recommends that this practice of de facto secrecy be eliminated. We recommend to the Frankfort School Board that its meetings start earlier and end earlier and that no meeting last beyond 11 p.m. If the necessary business cannot be accomplished by that time, then the board should meet on another night.

Parents, interested citizens and other taxpayers have a right to know what is going on and a right to participate in their government. We urge the Frankfort School Board to recognize these rights.

Lights dim, sounds blast — Matt rolls

Frankfort *Times*, June 21, 1972

Senate and gubernatorial candidates in Indiana formerly were chosen in party conventions — exciting, boisterous, wheeling-and-dealing affairs. *Times* publisher John E. Mitchell had been a state representative and had worked for former governors Matt Welsh and Roger Branigin. Mitchell, who had the best political mind of anyone I have known, suggested that I cover the Democrat and Republican conventions for Nixon Newspapers.

After sitting out eight years (governors were limited to one term in those days), Welsh decided to run for a second term. Here's my news/analysis piece on his winning the nomination.

INDIANAPOLIS — Suddenly, the lights went low and the sound system was captured.

Matt Welsh was on his way.

There weren't supposed to be any jazzed-up demonstrations at this year's Democratic State Convention, and for a while, it looked as if the Welsh forces would comply.

Through the opening, humdrum hours, Larry Conrad seemed to be gaining ground in a final desperation drive for the gubernatorial nomination.

But while the huge Conrad signs overshadowed the Welsh placards in the gallery, the Welsh lieutenants were keeping it all together on the floor — and it is on the floor, where the delegates are, that nominations are won. Conrad's demonstration was brief, enthusiastic, lively, noisy, rather impressive in light of the low-key activity that had preceded it.

Then South Bend Mayor Jerry Miller nominated Welsh, and, as

his final word was spoken, the lights dimmed and the powerful sound system in the convention hall blasted forth with "Happy Days Are Here Again."

The delegates on the floor responded, their flying hands and arms making movable shadows, and across the way, a high school band, complete with a pom-pon chorus, went into melodic action.

"We want Matt! We want Matt! We want Matt!"

Conrad forces against the far wall of the building tried to respond with "We want Larry!" — but this was former Governor Welsh's time, and neither gavel pounding nor Conrad backers were about to steal it.

The Welsh extravaganza over, the gallery gang settled back to pretzels, beef sandwiches, popcorn, apples, potato chips, sausage sandwiches and soft drinks, punctuating bites with words of disgust for the service.

Indications were that it was taking up to one hour to get waited on, and a woman from Martinsville wanted to know why vendors couldn't circulate through the bleachers, like they do at ballgames.

Others, too impatient or too tired to wait in line, read newspapers or went visiting as the nominations for attorney general got underway.

One woman dipped into her "Matt Pack," a plastic bag that contained a referee's whistle, a newspaper hat, a balloon and various pieces of literature. Out came the balloon in exchange for the whistle that she had earlier given to her young son.

The fireworks for Matt were over — and who needs shrill whistles all day?

Meanwhile, for others, it was a time for people-watching — and one strange sight for Clinton and Boone County Democrats was to see Republican John Donaldson of Lebanon, who represents both counties in the House, stroll by the fringes of the area.

Donaldson, wisely, was not wearing a pair of pants he often sports, the pair bedecked with tiny elephants.

Then came a first — the reading of partial returns as they began to flow to the speaker's rostrum after being tallied by the State Board of Accounts.

In the past, it was sudden death for the candidate who didn't make it — but now it would be slow death for Conrad. Welsh's final margin was 497 — 1,318 to 821 — and while there might have been some Welsh backers who figured on a larger spread, sadness was hard to spot on the faces of people who wore Welsh badges.

A short time later, history. Theodore Wilson, the attorney general hopeful, beat his three opponents on the first ballot to become the first Black nominated for a state office.

Later, as the cigar smoke thickened and apple cores could be spotted here and there among the debris, Welsh and Conrad came down the center aisle together, front and center.

Said Conrad, who still has a job as secretary of state, "I found out I could take a lickin' and keep on tickin'."

A teenager in the gallery, who wore a Welsh straw hat, carried a Conrad placard and had cheered loudly for the black Mr. Wilson, smiled broadly.

Then it was Welsh — in trim blue suit, blue shirt, red, white and blue-stripped tie — and while the words brought no great huzzahs, the response was solid, true, and you could sense the confidence in the sparkling new hall.

So the Democrats had their man, the custodians a huge room to clean and the Republicans a few hours left before they get to do their thing.

Bowen, Bulen in 10-second drama

Frankfort *Times*, June 24, 1972

A few days after the Democrat convention, the Republicans met to nominate a gubernatorial candidate among five men, including Speaker of the House Dr. Otis Bowen. He was favored, even though Keith Bulen, the National Committeeman from Indiana and the state's most powerful political operative, was backing Judge William Sharp.

After Bowen was nominated on the first ballot, I wandered to the rear of the stage just in time to see Bowen say farewell to a few well-wishers. His back was to me as he bent into a squatting position. Bulen was facing me as he approached Bowen.

I was right next to Bowen's right side and essentially alone with the two men when I caught their brief exchange. It was a telling moment in Indiana politics — one that some readers didn't believe. A few weeks after the convention, I received a signed photo from Bulen showing Bowen, himself and me. Bulen signed the photo and praised my story. I now had proof if I needed it. I never did.

INDIANAPOLIS — Dr. Otis Bowen sat on his haunches, his body balanced on the balls of the his feet, and greeted a tiny knot of well-wishers.

The scene was a back corner edge of the stage that fronted the convention hall, where a few minutes earlier Bowen had won a rousing first-ballot victory for the Republican gubernatorial nomination.

A handshake here, a handshake there, lots of smiles, and words of appreciation flowed from the Bremen physician.

Then, out of nowhere, a familiar face appeared, tired and taut.

It belonged to a man named Keith Bulen.

"Good luck and congratulations," Bulen said softly.

"Thank you," Bowen said, just as softly.

Bulen quickly moved on, the 10-second drama over.

The reception had not been jovial — but it was far from cool.

Otis Bowen and Keith Bulen know that they need each other — and so do the Republican pros who want to keep the governor's chair come November.

Although Bulen never directly endorsed one of the four governor candidates, it was openly known that he did not favor Bowen and leaned toward Judge William Sharp of Owen County.

But Bowen is a strange combination of a man — for a politician. He is gentle and not vindictive, and he knows what must be done to win.

He knows he needs Marion County big in November, to offset the strong Democrat vote in Lake County — and he knows Keith Bulen can deliver Marion County better than anyone.

Bowen also knows that while Bulen suffered a rare defeat, Bulen is still a strong political force in the Hoosier GOP.

Others on the floor of the center knew it, too.

One county chairman put it this way: "He just couldn't get a combination working for him."

And another political veteran added: "Bulen sacrificed his own vanity and image, because he couldn't get on the Bowen bandwagon. He knew all along Doc was in, but there was always (governor) Whitcomb breathing down his neck."

Still another pro defended Bulen by attacking Whitcomb's closest confidante, attorney Don Tabbert. The man said:

"Tabbert wants to control, Bulen just wants to have you listen, and there's a difference. Keith is still the smartest when it comes to maneuvering."

Then Clinton County Chairman James T. "Tom" Robison, a state representative who did not seek re-election, put in the final glowing words for Bulen:

"Keith got caught in a candidate sandwich. You can't 'operate' every year. But the important thing is, he did something for the party awhile back that few people know about and understand. He got the party back together."

A reporter asked Robison to explain, and he did.

"I sat in the home of a prominent Frankfort farmer one night with Keith, and he told how John Mitchell, when he was still attorney general, told him to get Indiana back together again.

"You'll remember, there was all that fighting among John Snyder — he was chairman then — and Whitcomb and Tabbert and the others.

"Well, Keith did it. He got the mess straightened out."

And so will Bulen now work hard for Bowen?

"Sure," Robison replied. "He and J.B. King, Doc's campaign manager, have never stopped talking. And they've been friends for a long time."

The brief Bowen-Bulen meeting at the back of the stage might not have been jovial, but apparently there was warmth and meaning in it — and both men understood it.

Gas strike not for him, but ...

Frankfort *Times*, September 18, 1973

As this book was being put together, gas prices were soaring, causing economic hardship throughout the country. It's not the first time gas prices have been a major issue.

In June 1973, President Richard Nixon ordered Phase IV price controls designed to control inflation. He said, "Phase 4 measures will stabilize both the prices at the retail level of food and the price of gasoline at your service station."

Prices had increased so sharply at some service stations, operators were threatened with violence, which prompted this column about one station who was trying to hold down prices. The station owner asked not to be identified, for obvious reasons.

If it comes down to the gun or the knife or the rock or the tire iron — he'll close.

He operates a service station.

And like fellow operators throughout the nation, he doesn't like living these days with Phase 4 price controls.

But he will stay open in Frankfort, and he thinks most other stations will, too.

He is worried about the current state of gasoline affairs, but he takes a common sense and rather calm attitude about the situation.

"I can't see any reason to close," he says, flicking ashes off his cigarette. "I don't think that is the way to go about this thing."

But if the threat of violence from other operators rears its ugly head, he will close.

"I'm not going to hassle with anybody if they start threatening me," he says evenly.

And he says he won't fight with his oil company — one of the major ones — if it decides to boost its prices again. The last time was in May, and he's been "able to live with it so far."

The sale of gasoline, he notes, never has been a money-making venture.

"It's about a break-even proposition," he says. "I mean, when you start figuring the paper towels for wiping down the windows, the electricity used, the labor — these guys get around $3 an hour — the air for tires, the insurance ...

"I would say that 75 percent of all my insurance is for the driveway. You have traffic moving in and out all day long. You have to have the protection."

The profit in the service station business comes from the inside work — lubes, oil changes, mechanical repair — and accessories.

But despite the break-even aspect of pumping gas, he says he wants to keep right on doing it. And he worries about talk of a nationwide shutdown of stations.

"Do you realize what it could do to the country?" he asks, lighting another cigarette.

"A major shutdown could break the country. If you don't get gas, you don't go — let's face it.

"And I would bet that service stations as a whole account for the largest tax bite in the country. Eight cents comes off every gallon to the state and another four cents goes to the federal government. On top of that, there's the four-cent sales tax in Indiana."

He took a pen from his pocket and began scribbling figures on a carton that encased cans of motor oil.

"If you figure the average station around here pumps 60,000 gallons a month, and there are about 15 stations, and 14 cents in taxes off each gallon ..." His hand flew, putting down the figures. "That's about $126,000 a month in taxes just in this small community alone."

He dragged on the cigarette. "What are we talking about in dollars when we talk about Indianapolis?"

He rolled on: "And what about all the unemployment that would be created? How would people get to work out of town, to Lafayette and Indianapolis and Kokomo?

"If the stations in this country closed for 30 days, the government would be broken."

What can be done?

"Well," and there is a faint smile, "we should get rid of Nixon and all those people around him. It's not just gas. It's meat and the farming situation. He's had bad advisors. I'm not a Republican or a Democrat; I vote for the man, and I voted for Nixon last time, but ..."

He gets off politics: "It's hard to manipulate the price of gas and the allocation of gas at the same time. You have to have a certain percentage of markup or you can't make it. I'll bet there are some guys working like dogs and making about a $1 a hour after all their overhead is taken care of. I'm doing OK for now, but there are others getting hurt."

After more than 30 minutes of discussion he still talks evenly, sensibly and a note of optimism tumbles from his mouth:

"It will all straighten itself out. I've been with this company for 12 years. The oil companies can't afford to put stations out of business. We're worth money to them, whether we sell the gasoline or not. Once they have unloaded it to us, they've made money."

And so he will keep pumping gas — and he will try to serve his customers the best way he can. He won't charge for wiping windows or putting in air or checking the oil — like some dealers have warned.

But if he is threatened with violence, then he will close. And:

"If I close, it will be for good."

Egyptians stress impact of 'new' Suez Canal

Nixon Newspapers, June 1974

In the spring of 1974, a New York travel agent with ties to the Middle East organized what she called The First Editorial Conference on the Middle East. This was shortly after the October 1973 War. Thirty press groups sponsored the tour, whose general theme was "Prospects of Peace in the Middle East."

Nixon Newspapers sent me on the tour. I represented the smallest newspapers among the 90 journalists, which included a few from broadcast media. (My roommate was a producer for NBC.) I wrote a 14-part series that — to my relief, more than satisfaction — won significant praise.

This story chronicles an incredible day in Egypt.

ALONG THE SUEZ CANAL — Overhead, an American helicopter breezes above the clear blue waters of the Suez Canal, periodically sending up an explosive spray after electronically detecting and then detonating a mine.

Below, an Egyptian general's remarks to a group of American journalists — perhaps the first to enter an area where fierce fighting took place only a few months ago — are occasionally drowned out by the chopper.

The action in the sky is part of Operation Nimbus Star, designed to clean the canal and restore traffic in one of the world's most important waterways.

The action below, under a tent that protects the journalists from 100-degree heat but not attacking flies, can be called Operation Public Relations.

Both are important to the Egyptians as they try to take advantage of their surprise showing in the 1973 October War.

Clearing the canal, shut down since the 1967 war, could mean as much as $250 million annually to Egypt, much needed cash as Cairo plans new economic growth.

The importance to the world is even more staggering. A United Nations report estimates $10 billion has been lost to higher shipping costs and lost trade since the Canal's closure.

Reopening the Suez, which is expected to take another 18 months, will mean that a third of the world's tanker fleet can shorten the distance from Persian Gulf petroleum fields to Mediterranean ports by at least two weeks.

The United States is playing a major role in clearing the waterway by providing $25 million and some 500 demolition and naval experts — despite the fact that Russia will benefit tremendously by the reopening. The Soviet navy's supply lines from Black Sea bases to the Straits of Malacca, door to the Pacific and Japan, will be reduced from more than 10,000 miles to about 2,200.

Israel, too, would benefit from the canal reopening — but when Egyptian officials were asked whether Israel will be allowed passage, they would only say it is an "international waterway" and make no commitment.

Egyptian leaders would rather talk about their plans for the "new" canal. Cairo hopes to widen and deepen the waterway — which runs 103 miles from Port Said to Port Tawfik — so that super tankers will be able to pass through. Prior to 1967, only ships up to 70,000 tons were able to navigate it.

By improving the canal, Egypt could double what was earned before the '67 war closed traffic.

Reopening the canal is crucial to a broader picture of general development, including the reconstruction of such important towns as Port Said, Suez City and Ismailia. Billions of dollars will be needed to accomplish the job.

After being briefed on the 1973 October War, the journalists were led from the tent back to buses to visit the war zone and canal cities, in ruins since 1967. On the way to Al Kantarah, on the canal's east bank, they had time to reflect on what had been said by Egyptian generals:

— That from a military point of view, the Egyptians knew Israel had three key strengths — rapid mobilization power, a strong air force and good armor.

— That Egypt felt it had to achieve surprise — and succeeded by striking on Yom Kippur, the holiest day in the Jewish year.

— That Israeli strongpoints would be attacked first by Egyptian soldiers coming across by boat — after artillery had wiped out mines — to battle Israeli tanks on foot while bridgeheads for tanks were being built between the strongpoints. By boat, it takes only seven minutes to cross the 400-foot canal.

It was an impressive public relations effort. It showed that Egypt had planned for months to attack and how. It showed, too, that Egypt had achieved much success. And the American journalists couldn't avoid being impressed — despite the Egyptians refusing to say how many men they lost, despite the generals admitting that Israeli forces along the canal were outnumbered 80,000 to 12,000 and despite the generals saying only, "That's another question," when asked why they didn't go deeper into the Sinai Desert.

Soon the bus reached Al Kantarah, which had 50,000 people before Israel mutilated it in 1967. The Egyptians regained it in October, in the process of killing some 300 Israeli reserves, after sweeping past the initial 70 men stationed at four strongpoints along the canal, near the city.

Al Kantarah's destruction seems less imposing compared with the damage inflicted on the larger "twin cities" of Suez and Port Tawfik to the south.

Buildings in those two cities were more modern. The journalists saw that every structure had been hit — starting with the '67 war, continuing with the war of attrition '67 to '70 and culminating last October.

The sight reminds one of tornado havoc in an Indiana community — only much worse.

Slowly the rubble is being removed and life is beginning to creep back to normalcy. Hundreds of people were killed in the 1967 war; those who survived we're evacuated to other Egyptian cities and villages. Now some people have returned, and they watch with deep interest as the journalists walk through the dust and debris to a building safe enough for occupancy.

Inside, the public relations effort continues. It is late and the journalists are hot, tired and thirsty. The Egyptians' Third Army commander smiles and explains that the buses have run out of gas and need to be refueled. Huge bottles of cold beer are brought out.

The army commander asks the journalists their opinion on political matters, but an Indiana newsman says politely, "General, we only report the news, not make it." The general laughs, understands.

Three hours later, after seeing acre after acre of sand, the journalists return to Cairo at 9:30. They have been gone since 7:30 a.m.

Most are struck by many things after spending four days in Egypt: a lack of arrogance from government and military chiefs, a sincere sense of friendship from the man in the street, a noticeable effort to improve U.S. relations as a major step toward economic growth, a solid job of public relations — and a reminder that war is hell.

HRC — people, love, rebirth

Frankfort *Times,* Nov. 7, 1974

I believe that this column is one of the best I ever wrote. Actually, the piece wrote itself.

Your eyes get wet and there isn't anything you can do about it.

But so what — they're tears of joy.

They sat at long tables, eating the baked steak, cooked carrots, bread, mashed potatoes and cottage cheese with peaches — and as you watched them, getting the nutrition they need while slicing away a piece of loneliness from their lives, it made your day.

The Paul Phillippe Human Resource Center.

Before going through the food line, about 60 senior citizens heard Rev. Charles Burgen, the center's director, say grace.

"We pray that today will be a good day for us and a good day for you, God," the minister said.

Simple words, but so meaningful, the kind of words He hears and does something with. Go to the center some day and ask the people who have found new lives there.

"You know," Chuck Burgen said as the line began moving forward, "this is not just a place for welfare people and the destitute. People have to understand this. This is a place for people. Lonely people."

He spoke the truth.

A man in a spiffy blue suit joked with a woman in front of him — and you got the feeling that the man always came to the center neat and clean and dressed nicely, that this was not some special occasion for him.

It wasn't a special occasion for anyone. It was just another day in the week when senior citizens could come to the center and eat the kind of food essential to their bodies — instead of making do at home with a bowl of cereal or a peanut butter sandwich.

You wonder where all these people spent their time before the center got rolling earlier this year. You ask, and the answer is simple.

"They spent their time at home, watching television and dying," said Aileen Ford, one of the assistant directors.

For some of them, the center has become more than just a place to visit with friends, to get a solid meal, to have fun, to spend their years without life's little worries and fears nagging them.

Go visit some day and ask about the center's 73-year-old cook, a woman who baked for thousands of Purdue students for years, before beginning to fade into bad health and senility. Go ask and be surprised.

Others help their less fortunate peers by taking food to them.

A woman in her 70s tells about how a woman in a wheel chair pulled her down and hugged her and kissed her when a hot meal was brought to the home.

Said the woman in her 70s: "We have to help them. Some day we'll be old." There was only a half-smile on her face and her words were not totally in jest.

You had to laugh — and almost reach for your handkerchief.

"Oh, we had fun here yesterday," the woman continued. "We had a Halloween party."

Earlier, Aileen Ford and Rev. Burgen's wife, Ann, talked about the party, relating how some people even kept their faces hidden behind their masks while they ate. "They would just lift up the mask enough to get the food into their mouth," Aileen Ford chuckled.

It is clear that Aileen Ford, a registered nurse who specializes in health services, and Kay Metzer, the other assistant director, who specializes in social activities, get something special from their jobs. How can they and others who work there miss?

How can they when, on the day the center celebrates birthdays, they watch the "birthday boy" or "birthday girl" get up and take a minute to talk about their life?

They can't — because before them is a human being, and for once, other human beings, who understand all too well, are listening, giving their undivided attention.

Hey, I'm sorry if I wore it on my sleeve today.

But listen, drop over to South Second Street. See for yourself.

A Christmas that tops them all

Frankfort *Times*, Dec. 24, 1974

A Christmas column that invokes the true meaning of the day.

She is old enough now to understand why that Christmas 10 years ago will always be special.

Christine Woolfington began putting the pieces together three years ago, and now she knows that she came close to being a motherless infant.

Except for a double cleft palate, Christine came into the world smoothly on a June day in 1964. Mom was fine too — but nine days later Jane Woolfington began hemorrhaging.

Her doctor, the late Fred Flora, assisted by Harry Stout and George Hammersley, tried two D and C's, a scraping of the uterus' lining that often stops the bleeding.

No luck. Hammersley would have to do a relatively new kind of surgery to stop the hemorrhaging. It came on a Saturday night.

Then, early Sunday morning, it was discovered that the local blood bank was depleted of Jane's type A-positive blood. She had already received eight pints in 72 hours.

It was too late to get a supply from the Fort Wayne Regional Blood Center, so the hospital turned to the Red Cross, which supplied a list of previous A-positive donors.

Enter four men — Larry Camp, Virgil Dowden, Bob Behr and Dick Woolridge.

Camp, who lived then at 659 Blinn Ave. but now resides in Bringhurst, remembers that 4 a.m. experience well.

"My wife answered the phone," he begins, "and she was, of course, half asleep. She knows I hate to be woke up, so at first she told the nurse she wouldn't wake me. But then, as she began to wake up, she understood and woke me up. I was mad, but when I found out, I went right out."

Camp, who didn't know the Woolfingtons, later got a Christmas card with some warm words of thanks tucked inside.

Dowden, who lives at 1701 E. Jefferson, didn't know the Woolfingtons either. "They didn't tell me what it was for," he recalls today. "At first, I thought maybe one of my kids — they were teenagers — was in an accident. The hospital just said, 'Would you give blood?' and I said, 'Yeah, sure.' I threw on my clothes and took off."

Behr was not acquainted with Jane either, but he had gone to school with her father-in-law, Eugene Woolfington. Behr took the call, listened to the request, "never gave it much thought" and got dressed to do something at 4 in the morning that many people never do once in their life.

Woolridge had gone to school with Jane's brother and sisters, and to this day occasionally sees and talks to her. He didn't hesitate either, but for a moment he got a shock he'll never forget.

"They said they needed blood for Janie, and we had an 8-year-old daughter named Jane," Woolridge explains. "Of course, she's 18 now. For a second, I was scared, and then I realized it wasn't for her. That's why I remember the whole thing so well."

Later that Sunday, Jane's plight was announced in church, and she points out today that some people went right to the hospital and donated blood in her name.

Dr. Flora said at the time that "without the blood, Mrs. Woolfington would not have made it. There's no question that blood transfusions saved her life."

So six months later, the true meaning of Christmas hit Mike Woolfington full force — the gift of life, a daughter six months old and a wife now a bit weak but fully recovered.

"That Christmas still stands out over other Christmases," Jane said the other day during a visit from Plymouth, where Mike is associated with Warner Corp., selling livestock and poultry equipment.

"There are so many different reasons. Of course, being healthy enough to take care of the baby. And by that time she was adjusting to the cleft palate problem. We knew that by the time she was 18 months, she would have to have surgery, but I had in my mind that she would be all right. She was strong.

"And that Christmas reminded me how wonderful people and friends could be. They were right there when we needed them, because, like I had three surgeries in one night. "

Three years later, Craig Woolfington came along after a normal pregnancy. "Everybody was kind of worried," Jane says, "but they took extra precautions and everything was fine. Craig weighed almost 10 pounds."

Soon he will learn about the events of 1964 and begin to understand life better.

Tomorrow, he'll celebrate Christmas with his sister and his parents. And while tomorrow promises to be a great day for them, it probably won't quite come up to one 10 years ago.

How could it?

'America's most trusted man' speaks his mind

Wabash Plain Dealer, Nov. 22, 1976

Walter Cronkite was 60 and still at his peak when I got an exclusive interview with him in Wabash.

The Wabash Valley Music Association, a non-profit group, brought Cronkite to town. Cronkite was booked to appear Nov. 20, 1976, for "A Lincoln Portrait" with the Indianapolis Symphony Orchestra.

Howard Garver, a retired executive with General Tire, Wabash's largest employer at the time, was the point man for the association. He also was a close friend of Joe and Marian Nixon, who were major supporters of the concert series. He had taken a liking to me.

After the schedule of 1976 performances was announced, newspapers and television stations surrounding Wabash requested interviews with Cronkite. Garver denied their requests. Some news outlets squawked, but Garver held firm. He had decided that Nixon Newspapers' "chief editor," as he referred to me, should interview Cronkite exclusively.

After Cronkite did his thing, and while the Indianapolis Symphony Orchestra continued to perform, *Wabash Plain Dealer* photographer Harold Chatlosh and I were escorted backstage. "Uncle Walter" greeted us warmly in a small office.

Three weeks after my story ran, Joe Nixon received a brief "Dear Joe" letter from Cronkite. Joe gave me a copy. The first paragraph reads:

"I thought Ray Moscowitz's article and indeed the entire coverage and pictures in the *Wabash Plain Dealer* was as fine a journalistic effort as I have seen anywhere. It put the icing on a most delightful evening in your fair city."

Of course, Cronkite's words delighted me — for about five minutes.

He is sorry Richard Nixon was President.

The four major problems facing the world today are pollution, population, depletion of natural resources and nuclear proliferation.

If campaign laws were made so candidates didn't have to "beg" for funds, he would consider a Senate race.

Those are opinions you won't hear on the CBS Evening News with Walter Cronkite. And that's to be expected when you're considered the most trusted man in America — an honor that has been bestowed on the 60-year-old Cronkite.

Off-camera, though, Cronkite freely gives his views, as he did here Saturday night after performing "A Lincoln Portrait" with the Indianapolis Symphony at Honeywell Center.

Our chat in Building Supt. Joe Kendall's office began with Cronkite pouring a glass of water. Looking rather handsome in his tuxedo, he plopped himself on the corner of the couch, a relaxed and gracious figure.

In a 1970 *Look* magazine interview with Italian journalist Oriana Fallaci, Cronkite wouldn't answer when she asked if he was glad Nixon was President.

But Saturday night there was no hesitation from America's No. 1 television news anchorman, whose audience averages almost 11 million homes each weeknight.

"There was a conspiracy to muzzle us (the media) — and I was proven right after I made that claim," Cronkite said when asked about the Nixon-Spiro Agnew bout with the press that began after Nixon was elected in 1968.

"Some of my fellow journalists said I was seeing ghosts under the bed, but Watergate provided the documentation to prove that I was right."

But while Cronkite feels Nixon tarnished the office of the presidency, he sees a silver lining in the Nixon crisis, "because the net effect was that the first test of our system showed that it really works, that the checks and balances will work. The legislative, judiciary and press bodies all played their parts."

Cronkite thinks Gerald Ford deserves much credit for "helping us recover from the horrible siege of Watergate."

He took a sip of water-and continued: "Ford deserves the credit he mentioned himself. He brought back a sense of stability with skill after Watergate and Vietnam."

Did Ford's performance surprise him?

"Yes, he probably did better than I thought he would. Most occupants of the White House rise to the office."

Now Jimmy Carter.

"And I'm glad," Cronkite smiled, "because now we can show after eight Republican years that we can be just as tough on the Democrats."

Asked to comment on Carter, Cronkite responded: "It's hard to see the shape his administration will take. It's going to be interesting as a newsman — it's going to be exciting if he moves on all fronts as he suggested during the campaign."

Carter has many promises out to many people, Cronkite noted, "and to balance the budget and do all the things he wants to do will require some innovative proposals. It will be interesting to see if he can achieve his desire to make the bureaucracy more efficient."

No matter which direction Carter's administration takes, Cronkite will strive to present the news as objectively as he can. He admits there is probably a bit more pressure to report as fairly, clearly and straightforward as possible because of being described by *Time* magazine as "the single most convincing and authoritative figure in television news."

Asked how he felt when told a survey showed he was the most trusted man in America, Cronkite chuckled: "I thought the country was in trouble."

Cronkite continued in a modest vein: "I guess it (most trusted) comes from longevity. Longevity gives one a feeling of authority. Obviously, it (most trusted) has some effect on me. I want to be sure that my integrity is not tarnished. But I think all newsmen do the best they can, are as unbiased as they can be."

Cronkite also feels that because he does not — will not — do commentaries like his CBS colleague, Eric Sevareid, NBC's David Brinkley, ABC's Harry Reasoner and others, people have come to believe him more. A journalist can't do 21 minutes of straight reporting on the air and then 2 minutes of commentary, he asserted.

"We know we can write a 2-minute piece and turn off our prejudices for 21 minutes, but people aren't that sophisticated to see it," he said.

"They can't see the difference between opinion and fact."

Cronkite's views — past and present — might come forth some day in his memoirs. If they do, here are some opinions he will probably expound on:

— Henry Kissinger has been brilliant in his negotiations, "but I don't particularly agree with him on foreign policy. His big nation balance of power policy is retrogressive. It's necessary to achieve big nation rapprochement — China was good. But along with that we need a parallel policy of moving ahead with international law. We have to make the United Nations work." He thinks Kissinger might become the "Averill Harriman of the next generation" — a world statesman taking on special negotiating roles, such as in the Mideast.

— Dwight Eisenhower was a better president than generally given credit for, "because he did nothing and did it well at a time when that was needed. He was effective because he wanted to calm the country and bring it back from World War 2."

— It's a tossup between Nixon and Harry Truman on the president who did the best job in foreign affairs. He cited Nixon's China role, Truman's Marshall Plan.

— Lyndon Johnson was the best president in getting legislation passed, particularly domestic programs.

— Two world leaders who have particularly impressed him in face-to-face interviews are Yugoslavia's Tito — "he was so vigorous for a man his age" — and Egypt's Anwar Sadat for the courage he has shown in Mideast negotiations.

So much for Cronkite views. What about the man, himself?

— He would think about a Senate race if he didn't have to "beg for campaign funds and then have to be beholden to people. I wouldn't want to feel obligated."

— When he's not working he likes sailing, tennis, reading and "good bull sessions with fellow journalists or reasonably intelligent people."

— His peeves center mostly around people who are discourteous, boorish, intolerant and inefficient.

— He wouldn't be surprised if some day CBS provided him with a co-anchor person. "There's no talk about it. I'm not in favor of it for a 30-minute broadcast; it's too awkward a form for a half-hour. A co-anchor for a one-hour broadcast, however, would be all right, and probably necessary, because it might be too difficult for one person to handle."

After an hour of face-to-face conversation, it was clear that Cronkite, who has been in journalism for 44 years — he joined CBS in 1950 — has not lost any enthusiasm for his work.

It is an enthusiasm that began when Cronkite was in junior high school and he read *The American Boy* magazine series of short stories on careers. Only two careers drew his interest — mining engineering and journalism. It is an enthusiasm that will carry him well for the next five years, before CBS' mandatory retirement age takes effect.

And, as Walter would say, that's the way it is.

'Music is endless,' Goodman says — and he should know

Wabash Plain Dealer, Feb. 9, 1977

On a Friday morning, Merv Hendricks, the managing editor of the *Wabash Plain Dealer*, came into my office around 9:45. At the time I was the executive editor of Nixon Newspapers but was not involved in day-to-day operations.

"Could you do me a favor?" he asked.

"Yeah, sure," I said.

"My reporters are too young to write about Benny Goodman. ... Would you write a piece for today's paper?"

"Yeah, sure," I replied.

Hendricks said that Goodman was expecting me and photographer Harold Chatlosh at the Holiday Inn.

Here's the piece I wrote on deadline.

"Music is endless."

The words are Benny Goodman's — and he should know.

"I'm always working at it, always studying," he said in a soft, slightly raw voice this morning, lounging back on a Holiday Inn couch, his feet resting on the plain brown coffee table.

At 67, Goodman is a legend, a man generally considered as the father of swing, a hot rhythmic jazz sound that came pouring forth in 1935 and captured the nation.

And tonight, when Goodman plays at Honeywell Center for a packed Wabash Valley Music Association crowd, he'll stick to the music that shaped his greatness. He doesn't know what he'll play, he said, but look for Airmail Midnight Special, Body and Soul and the classic Sing, Sing, Sing.

He'll be joined by six others — the great Buddy Tate on sax, newcomer Cal Collins on guitar, Warren Vache on trumpet, John Bunch on piano, Connie Kay on drums and a guy named Totah on bass.

"I can't remember his first name," Goodman smiled.

Remembering the music won't be any trouble, though, and the hot improvisation that provides swing with its soul will flow forth naturally, too.

Unlike some great artists who continue to perform deep into their lives, Goodman must contend with the physical requirements necessary for his craft. Simply standing and playing his instrument is tough on any performer, especially when he's constantly on the road, living out of suitcases and motel rooms.

But Goodman swings on, and when he's asked where the old pepper comes from, where his enthusiasm is derived, he looks almost bewildered.

It is clear Goodman is still having a ball, that he is still searching for different sounds, that the drive that was instilled in him at age 10 is still pulsating.

Even today he is commissioning new music from such renowned writers as Gordon Jenkins and Malcomb Arnold, who wrote the beautiful score for the movie "Bridge on the River Kwai."

"You've got to stir things up," he said, tugging at his gray slacks, revealing long gray woolen socks inside brown slippers. You've got to keep looking for things, trying different things."

Goodman has been studying and looking and trying for more than 40 years — a span of time in which he has performed with the greatest jazz musicians of all time.

Asked to name an "all star" team of jazz, he laughed lightly and hesitated only for a moment before spilling out some names.

Without hesitation, he named Gene Krupa on drums and Teddy Wilson on piano. He needed a little coaching before naming Zoot Sims on sax. And he settled on Louis Armstrong and Bix Beiderbecke on trumpet. His bass man would be Israel Crosby. And when asked about trombone, he replied, "Say, you keep putting me on the spot," and then there was a soft laugh from a throat that's battling a slight cold.

And then, when asked who his favorite clarinet player is, he chuckled. Artie Shaw was okay. "And that fellow from New Orleans."

Pete Fountain?

"Yeah, he's a good honest player — not very inventive, but okay," came the reply.

What about his favorite piece of music?

The answer came quickly: "I have none. I have too many favorites."

So tonight, when Benny Goodman walks on the stage with his clarinet and his six fellow musicians, it's not certain what will come pouring forth.

But it's certain that it will be music that will always live in America, truly American music from a man who came out of the Chicago ghetto — the eighth of eleven children — and gave it lasting permanence.

Sen. Bayh bids farewell to Oval Office goal

Nixon Hoosier Feature Service, April 1977

This piece is one of eight in a series of articles called "Hoosiers in Washington," written for the Nixon Hoosier Feature Service that I created as executive editor for the group. The series was sold to several newspapers throughout Indiana, which resulted in wide distribution and lots of feedback.

This piece about Sen. Birch Bayh breaks some news: that he would not make another run for the presidency. Much of what Bayh said in the spring of 1977 has relevance today.

WASHINGTON — There will be no more runs for the presidency — and that's fine with Birch Bayh.

Don't get him wrong. Bayh's two tries for the nation's highest office were genuine, hard-charging attempts.

But after talking with him for an hour in his Russell Building office, it's obvious he's content being a senator — and satisfied he answered legitimate presidential calls twice.

"I can't think of anything else I'd rather do," he said when asked what his future would hold if he was not — now — Indiana's senior senator. "Maybe teach or practice law."

He chuckled as he rolled up his sleeves and loosened his tie: "I remember one Sunday not long ago hearing about some problem facing the President, and I said to myself, 'Well, I'm glad I don't have to worry about that.'"

Shortly after starting his third six-year term, in 1975, Bayh was pushed to make a second presidential bid. No Democrat had established himself. But when Bayh finally decided to run, it was too late. He admits he waited too long to gear up his election machinery.

The presidential push developed from Bayh's Senate record — a record that has grabbed nationwide attention. He sponsored the 25th Amendment, which clarifies presidential succession. He sponsored the Equal Rights Amendment, which needs three more states' approval for ratification. He fought the nominations of G. Harrold Carswell and Clement Haynesworth to the Supreme Court — and won. His latest project is Electoral College reform.

Others' absence from Congress has propelled Bayh even more into the forefront of the nation's legislative leaders: Indiana's former senior senator, Vance Hartke, Robert Taft Jr. of Ohio and William Brock of Tennessee were defeated; party leaders Mike Mansfield of Montana and Hugh Scott of Pennsylvania retired; Minnesota's Walter Mondale was elevated to the vice presidency, and Michigan's Philip Hart died.

Thus, Bayh's attention and views are sought even more today — as demonstrated by an outer office filled with people and word from his press secretary that all three television networks want to interview him.

Asked about his views, Bayh responded without hesitation in a relaxed, conversational tone.

—The economy: "All of our problems stem from this one," he began. "Even energy. And our social programs are affected by it. They depend on our ability to develop our resources. If we're not working, we don't have these resources, and so more people need social services. It's a double-headed monster.

"We have to get more off unemployment to solve our deficit situation. When you get people working, buying, selling, you are able to cut back on social services. We need to spend money on housing, sewer systems, wastewater treatment plants, so we can get people to put in a day's work and show something for it. We need to channel it through the private sector.

"We need to generate even more industry investment than normal. We need to free up the money supply — in the private sector — so farmers can buy tractors and newlyweds can think about buying homes."

— The oil companies: "I still feel we have to break the stranglehold a few large oil companies have on crude oil and refined petroleum products from the time oil is taken from the ground until it is sold to the consumer."

On a related issue, Bayh said he favors deregulation of natural gas. "I support deregulating new gas, but not old gas in the ground," he said. "I think some large corporations are keeping gas in the ground.

"People ought to go to jail if a massive supply of gas comes forth after a price increase — meaning people were gambling and sitting with supplies while some people in Indiana were cold this winter."

— Coal as a resource: "There are great coal deposits and we're getting close to getting the sulphur out economically. We ought to be pouring a lot of bucks into research. 95 percent of our energy research has gone to nuclear; almost nothing to solar and coal."

— Carter's stance on foreign dissidents: "He deserves support. We have to keep prodding the Russians. If this country can't be a spokesman for oppressed people, what country will? Most of our ancestors would have fallen into the category of dissident. They wanted to leave and go somewhere else."

— The $50 rebate: "I have mixed feelings. I suppose it's the best way to give the economy an immediate kick, and we need it, but not for the long run."

The conversation swung off the issues, and Bayh was asked what advice he would give — if any — to Indiana's freshman senator, Richard Lugar.

"He doesn't need any advice," Bayh responded. "He's been in government long enough to know how to handle himself." Bayh hesitated, looking down at the floor, then: "I came here with the idea that I didn't have all the answers. That's still true. I think Sen. Lugar understands that. There are few miracles; it's a lot of hard work, and it takes patience. You have to be able to take criticism, and he knows that."

Bayh said his relations with Lugar have been smooth, noting Lugar had co-signed with him and Rep. Floyd J. Fithian (D-Lafayette) letters petitioning the Soviet Union to permit the emigration of two Soviet citizens seeking to join their families in the United States and Israel. Bayh also asked Lugar to co-sign a letter to Defense Secretary Harold Brown urging support for a bill that would save jobs for Hoosiers working at the Crane Naval Support Center and other government installations.

"Legitimate jobs in maintenance, operations and weapons research should not be abolished," Bayh asserted.

Now the chief dispenser of federal patronage for Indiana, Bayh said he would advise Lugar on appointments. He arranged for Virginia Dill McCarty, named by Bayh for a U.S. Attorney post, to meet with Lugar.

"The practical facts are that with a Democrat president, you have Democrat people in the top spots, and vice versa," Bayh said with frankness. He added: "I can assure you, though, that the appointments made will be of the caliber that Sen. Lugar can be proud of. They will provide the kind of services needed."

There was a final question before Bayh moved on to other matters: Does being content as a senator mean he will seek re-election in four years?

"I can't think about that now," he replied. "I want to keep my options open."

Does he think Gov. Otis Bowen would run? "I have no idea on Doc," Bayh responded. "If he does, more power to him."

It was clear that those final words came from a man at peace with himself and his ability, locked into a feeling that he belongs in the U.S. Senate and is going to make the best of that opportunity.

Life's facets no stranger to treaty negotiator

Nixon Hoosier Feature Service, December 1977

At the semi-annual meeting of the Inland Press Association in 1977 in Chicago, Sol Linowitz, the lead negotiator for the Panama Canal Treaties, was the featured speaker at breakfast one day.

After he spoke, I quickly went to the head table and introduced myself. When he heard "Moscowitz," a smile crept across his face. I asked him if I could interview him in Washington. He gave me his card and told me to call his secretary.

On Thanksgiving eve 1977, I took an early-morning flight to Washington, interviewed Linowitz in his well-appointed office for more than an hour and flew back to Indiana that afternoon.

The result was this story for the Nixon Hoosier Feature Service, which had already pre-sold to several Indiana newspapers a profile on Linowitz and a Q&A.

WASHINGTON — He is into everything — running, driving, walking, flying — a human blotter absorbing the mainstreams of life.

Religion. Education. International relations. Media. Business. Finance. World order. Medicine. The arts.

What makes 63-year-old Sol Myron Linowitz run? And who is this man playing one of two major roles in the Panama Canal Treaties negotiations?

He is, simply, a deeply religious Jewish lawyer who says he can "never remember a time in my life when I wasn't doing things that involved and helped other people. I don't say this grandly. I just say it as a fact. Just a part of me — and it came from my family."

It was a family of four sons, headed by immigrant parents from

Austro-Poland who lived in Trenton, N.J. His father was a fruit importer before being wiped out by the Depression.

But limited family funds did not stop young Sol's drive for a higher education. He combined a scholarship and various jobs, including a violinist's role with the Utica Symphony Orchestra, to graduate with honors from Hamilton College in upstate New York.

Linowitz' Judaism has played a central role in his life. In college he considered becoming a rabbi.

"I guess I've always had a religious interest and bent," he said. "I found I got a lot out of my religion. I found things that my religion gave me which I thought I might helpfully communicate."

He decided against becoming a rabbi, but he's involved these days with them as the Jewish Theological Seminary's board chairman. Linowitz's Jewish heritage molds his philosophy of life.

"Judaism is basically a deep concern for other human beings. What I cherish is that it doesn't place me above other human beings, it doesn't tell me I'm better, it doesn't tell me I'm gifted or endowed or in any way given certain things that others ought not to have. And I do not get those things as a right."

He has tried to "deal fairly and justly with people in various situations ... I try to be thoughtful of other human beings."

The thoughtfulness comes through with sincerity when he's asked about Ronald Reagan, who has led the opposition to the Panama treaty.

"I like him very much," he said about Reagan. "We met twice for several hours on each occasion, and I found him open, cordial, gracious and civil and I thought penetrating in his questions and concerns. I enjoyed being with him. He had humor and wit."

Reagan raised several good questions, Linowitz said, and when the discussions concluded, Reagan said: "You have been responsive in every way and answered everyone of my questions. But we're going to come out on the opposite side."

Linowitz was able to successfully demonstrate that the United States could properly protect her national security, but the two men disagreed on the sovereignty issue, Linowitz said.

"The biggest point he made," Linowitz noted, "was about a concern

I think he genuinely feels. At a time when we have left Vietnam and talk about pulling out of South Korea, Reagan said, we seem to be in retreat ... that we will be seen in the eyes of the world as being pushed out by this 'little dictator down there,' as he put it, and won't earn the respect of the world ... that we'll be looked upon as weaklings because we have been threatened.

"I tried very hard to make clear to him that's not the case ... that after 14 years nobody is now suddenly threatening us ... that we inaugurated the negotiations and tried very carefully to work out terms that would be fair and reasonable. He admitted the terms we did work out were, as he put it, better than he thought could have been obtained."

Lenowitz talked about his negotiator's role.

"I took it on with a deep sense of responsibility, recognizing that this is an issue that has been in negotiation for 14 years. That it was filled with all kinds of implications for the future, not only between the United States and Panama, but this whole hemisphere.

"I think it's by far the most complicated thing I've ever undertaken in my life ... the toughest, the most demanding, and yet in some ways the most fulfilling."

Linowitz called on everything he had acquired in his life as a lawyer-businessman — he once was chairman of the board for Xerox Corp. — Judaic practitioner and diplomat.

"It all kind of came together," he said.

Now that the six-month appointment (that he requested when offered the job) has expired, where does private citizen (but still treaty consultant) Linowitz go from here?

"I will want to continue being involved as long as I'm able to be helpful. If somebody says to me, 'This is something that you uniquely can do,' then I'm going to try to do something about it. But that's the word — unique — that's important. I don't want to do what a lot of other people can do, because that, I don't think, is where I can make a particular contribution."

Finding that special something shouldn't be difficult. Linowitz serves on the boards of *Time* magazine, Pan American World Airways, Mutual Life Insurance Company of New York and three schools —

Johns Hopkins, Hamilton and Cornell. He's also involved with the Center for Inter-American Relations, The Trilateral Commission, the Council on Foreign Relations and the International Executive Service Corps.

And just for good measure, he's a trustee for the Salk Institute and a fellow of the American Academy of Arts and Sciences and the Royal Society of Arts.

So his "into everything" pace will continue, providing his health — bolstered by tennis, walking and watching what he eats — remains solid.

Why? Why when at his age and with such a full, rewarding life behind him he could relax and use his generous wealth for a variety of pleasures?

"I guess the simple answer is I have to," he says. "I want to use me best. There's so much to be done I wouldn't feel right for not doing these things. My wife and family (four daughters) are reconciled to it. I think they understand that's me, and they're not displeased that's me."

Is Dan Quayle the man to beat Bayh? He's not saying, but then again ...

Nixon Hoosier Feature Service, July 1978

This story got wide play via the Nixon Hoosier Feature Service. The Indianapolis News *did not run the story, but mentioned it in a political column that some political observers felt gave impetus to Quayle seeking a Senate seat. After two terms in the House of Representatives, Quayle ran for the Senate and upset Birch Bayh, who was seeking a fourth term.*

Could handsome, bright, conservative Dan Quayle unseat middle-aged, handsome, bright, liberal Birch Bayh?

Could Quayle succeed where such heavyweights as William Ruckelshaus and Richard Lugar failed?

Could Quayle score the same kind of upset he accomplished in 1976, when, as a political novice, he defeated veteran Democratic Congressman Ed Roush in the Fourth District?

Hoosier Republican strategists may be asking those questions after this November's general election.

A year ago, Gov. Otis Bowen was mentioned prominently as the GOP choice to face Bayh, who probably will seek a fourth term in 1980. But Bowen talk cooled after his wife suffered a bone disorder.

Although Bowen — the only man to win consecutive gubernatorial terms — hasn't ruled himself out, he hasn't sounded like a Senate contender either.

Which leaves the GOP field wide open — and tempting for Quayle.

At 31, Quayle is seeking a second House term against John Walda of Fort Wayne, who, like Quayle, is young, handsome, intelligent, connected with a newspaper family and an attorney.

Understandably, when Quayle is asked about a Bayh race, he says he's "more concerned with 1978 than 1980," adding: "Doc Bowen will beat Bayh hands down," sounding like a man who assumes the governor has decided to run.

That may be just political gamesmanship on Quayle's part. It doesn't mean 1980 hasn't entered his mind.

If it has, you can't blame him.

He has enjoyed an outstanding first term. When House leaders were asked to name six freshmen GOP congressmen they thought had a bright future, Quayle's name appeared on top of each list. And the *Chicago Tribune* featured Quayle and five other senators and congressmen as newcomers who have impressed Capitol-watchers.

Quayle, too, would have history on his side — no Hoosier has ever been elected to the Senate for four terms. In recent years, Bayh stopped Homer Capehart's bid for that distinction in 1962 and Lugar retired Vance Hartke in 1976 after three terms.

A Bayh-Quayle race would provide a clear-cut choice between a solid liberal and a solid conservative.

When Quayle relinquished his position as general manager of his family's newspaper, the *Huntington Herald-Press*, he went to Washington with some definite priorities:

— He wanted to study ways in which the federal bureaucracy could be reformed.

— He wanted to push for limited terms for House and Senate members to eradicate the seniority system and reduce lobbyists' influence.

— He wanted to balance the budget, battle inflation and cut taxes.

— He wanted to put "able-bodied" people to work through the private sector, not through such government programs as the Humphrey-Hawkins bill.

— He wanted to add his support to a strong military force.

Quayle has homed in on those priorities, despite running into a wall of frustration his first three months. Action moved too slowly. The committee system disappointed him.

Committee hearings are a farce, he said in an interview three months after taking office, because "the chairman can get a third of the committee to show up, get the proxies of those who don't and wind up with all the power."

Quayle adjusted, however, and by last January was telling people "...I'd have to say it's mostly the best of times right now."

Some frustration still lingers, though.

Listen:

"There just doesn't seem to be the commitment in Congress to deal with the federal bureaucracy. And President Carter seems to have softened on the issue, too. He seems to have resolved himself to the fact that no one administration is going to do anything about the cumbersome bureaucracy."

Quayle kept a campaign promise and fought the $13,000 Congressional pay raise.

When the pay increase passed, Quayle used some of it to start a program of bringing Fourth District high school seniors to Washington for a few days of learning and touring.

Constantly attacking "federal overgrowth," Quayle favors a recommendation made by Senate minority leader Howard Baker of Tennessee to cut legislative sessions in half.

"We would get paid about 50 percent of what we're paid now ($57,500)," Quayle said, backing Baker's call for Congress to meet from January to May and finish leftover legislation in the fall.

Only once has Quayle deserted the conservative fold on a major issue — the B1 Bomber.

Agreeing with Carter's decision to scrap the B1, Quayle said: "It is not a vital necessity. The cruise missile is more cost-effective, and it can get under radar."

But Quayle wouldn't back Carter's decision to reduce U.S. forces in South Korea.

On other key issues, Quayle:

— Voted against the Social Security tax, asserting it "was the largest peacetime tax placed upon the American people in our history. To have a secure Social Security trust fund, the financing should — one — include federal employees and — two — restore the integrity of the original intent of Social Security to that of a supplemental retirement income rather than the present welfare-laden program."

— Urged natural gas deregulation. "By increasing our production we would decrease our imports and move toward balance of payments surplus rather than a huge balance of trade deficit. If Congress does not deregulate gas, the consumer will ultimately pay more because of our reliance on the more expensive synthetic natural gas."

— Voted against the minimum wage increase, saying it adversely affects our inflation rate and causes unemployment, "particularly with youth, particularly youth minorities. "

— Claimed the House of Representatives should have had a voice in the Panama Canal Treaty ratification issue. He joined 50 other House members in a suit charging the treaties are invalid because the Constitution provides for the House and Senate to consent in transferring United States property. The Supreme Court refused to rule on the case and sent it back to the District Court of Appeals, which had said the suit "didn't have standing."

— Voted against the Consumer Protection Agency bill, arguing that "it would have established yet another layer of bureaucracy ... (calling) for more government and regulation rather than less."

— Voted consistently for tax cuts, opposing Carter's proposed $50 rebate (which the President eventually dropped). "Tax cuts will create more jobs and provide for the necessary economic expansion."

— Called for tax indexing, charging that "inflation is the most vicious tax we have today — an indirect tax you cannot see until you buy something at the store." Quayle and other congressmen propose linking the tax rate schedule and the standard deduction to the Consumer Price Index, "which will have the effect of eliminating tax increases generated as rising prices push individuals into higher tax brackets."

— Voted against the Humphrey-Hawkins bill (which calls for employment to get under 3 percent), asserting it is "the false promise of a quick cure for the nation's economic ills. Instead of creating government jobs, the Congress should be promoting ideas to provide employment in the private sector."

— Voted consistently in opposition to raising the national debt. "By having this huge deficit, the only logical economic result is continued high inflation."

— Voted with the majority as the House killed the common situs bill, which would have allowed secondary boycotts to shut down entire construction projects, "thus sparking more inflation and causing joblessness in the vital construction industry."

If Quayle's strong conservative views win a vote of confidence at Walda's expense in November, Quayle could catch the Senate bug.

He would have two years to put together the kind of organizational effort that propelled him past Roush.

In mid-July of 1976, still fresh from his primary success, Quayle saw poll figures which showed Roush far ahead, 61 to 27 percent. What's more, Quayle's name recognition factor registered a miniscule 13 percent.

Quayle and his wife, Marilyn, were disheartened by those figures, but he went into the political vineyards — the neighborhoods and the precincts — and quietly put things together.

His strong grassroots organization, his handsome face, his Indiana Law School degree, his experience working in state government with Attorney General Theodore Sendak, former Gov. Edgar Whitcomb and Gov. Bowen, his exposure via a series of televised debates with Roush and a minor third-party candidate — together those things produced the surprising triumph hardly anyone predicted.

Quayle hammered at Roush's liberal voting record — "it was 12 percent greater than Hartke's" — and attacked Roush on government spending.

If a Bayh-Quayle race materializes, the same formula will be used again.

So if GOP chieftains begin asking themselves if Quayle can unseat Bayh, it's understandable.

Also expectable.

Modern health care is real question

Wabash Plain Dealer, Oct. 20, 1978

This editorial got strong, positive feedback. The editorial urged the Wabash County Council — the folks in charge of spending — to support a hospital project in a forthcoming vote.

The hospital question that faces the County Council when it meets on Monday should be made clear: Does Wabash County need modernized hospital-health care facilities?

The question is not whether Wabash County should fight state and federal regulations.

Our answer to the question at hand is yes, modernized facilities are needed.

We raise the point in light of the council's 4-3 vote taken Oct. 10. That vote informally supported the $6.4 million project, allowing the plan to move through various state and regional administrative stages before final approval.

The three "no" votes were cast by Councilmen Joe Christle, Leon Ridenour and Roger Ranck, who asserted the county should challenge state and federal involvement in local matters.

We agree with Christle, Ridenour and Ranck that too much state and federal intervention can — at times — be frustrating and costly.

But to oppose the hospital project because outside agencies must be involved avoids the real question.

In voicing opposition, Councilman Ranck also said: "If I vote for this, I'm voting a lot of young families out of home ownership. I am in no way going to saddle the young people with an indebtedness of this type."

That argument raises these questions:

— What will county officials say to young parents with children who suffer from serious, complicated illnesses?

— What will county officials say to young parents whose child has fallen from a playground apparatus and needs proper emergency room care?

— What will county officials say to young families with aging parents in need of vital hospital services?

— What will county officials say to young families who find the job market stagnated because efforts to acquire new industry are partially hindered by a lack of modern hospital facilities?

Young families will not be denied home ownership by hospital indebtedness. Inflation is the main problem young families face — not excessive taxation — in seeking home ownership.

Again, when the council votes Monday on a resolution that gives formal support to the hospital plan, the central question should be whether modernized facilities are needed in Wabash County.

We hope Councilmen Christle, Ridenour and Ranck rethink their positions and help provide unanimous support for a project of crucial importance to our community's future.

Note: The editorial ran on a Friday. On Monday, the County Council voted on the resolution. In a 4-2 vote, the council approved a resolution calling for $4 million. Christle and Ranck again voted no. Ridenour left the meeting before the vote was taken.

A Journalist's Journey

Remember Jim Neal, GOP party healer?

Nixon Hoosier Feature Service, January 1979

One of the nicest and smartest guys I met in the newspaper business was Jim Neal, who also happened to have a first-rate political mind. I got the idea for this story one morning during the short drive to work.

NOBLESVILLE, Ind. — American Express hasn't asked Jim Neal to do a commercial. But if the credit card firm did, it would probably go something like this:

Framed by sketches of elephants and flanked by typewriters, the smallish, balding Neal would stand, coatless, glasses firmly in place, and in a semi-raspy voice that sounds like it needs a perpetual throat lozenge say:

"Do you know me?"

"Once upon a time, when Indiana's Republican Party didn't have the Good Doctor Bowen to heal its fratricide, I was asked to come out of this newsroom and into the GOP's sick bay ...."

That's just what happened six years ago — Jan. 13, 1972 — when Neal stopped being executive editor of the *Noblesville Daily Ledger* and became what one veteran political writer termed a U.N. peacekeeping force.

Neal had served 11 years as Republican State Central Committee secretary, so when asked to become interim state chairman and heal a bloody struggle between then-chairman John Snyder and Gov. Edgar Whitcomb, he was no amateur political tinkerer.

Neal swiftly bandaged the party machinery, resulting in a

remarkable achievement: Dr. Otis Bowen's 300,000-vote gubernatorial victory in 1972 over highly-respected former Gov. Matt Welsh. Neal remained chairman until Feb. 14, 1973, when the party's finances — $180,000 in debt when he assumed command — bathed in bucks. Then he rode off like the Lone Ranger.

So whatever happened to quiet, effective party-healer Jim Neal?

Nothing — he rode back to Noblesville to resume a newspaper career that has encompassed almost all of his 58 years as of today.

Neal, interviewed in his office adjacent to the *Ledger* newsroom, chuckles forth the truth when asked why the various GOP factions chose him:

"I never could pin it down. But I was told that Keith Bulen (then powerful Marion County chairman) and others listed every name they could think of. Then they began eliminating people and I was the last one left. It was a process of elimination."

It was much more than that. Neal knew every party leader, and as secretary he had not been in a policy position where his views could attract enemies.

What's more, the GOP chiefs knew Neal's orderly mind, sharpened by his student years at West Point and his military experience, was needed to reconstruct the party's nuts and bolts.

Honesty, too, was a factor in selecting Neal, who says, "You've got to tell the truth all the time. You have to be open, frank ... you can't dodge the issues. I have found that after sleeping on something over night and deciding I am wrong, I ought to be man enough to admit it."

So it's no surprise that Neal's comments about the Republican Party are straight forward, not sounding like a cheerleader only interested in slicing up Jimmy Carter and the Democrats.

He says bluntly: "The Republican Party is virtually dead now on the national level. We got a slight transfusion in November, but we haven't controlled Congress for over 40 years."

It bothers Neal that the GOP has not broadened its base. He points out that the Democrats "have moved to the right and stolen our thunder, but (Ronald) Reagan and the conservatives haven't moved at all."

Neal feels the Republicans would lose the 1980 presidential race with either Reagan or Gerald Ford against Carter, who he sees being re-nominated without any threat from Ted Kennedy or Jerry Brown.

"We made a mistake with Kemp-Roth (the Republican bill that would have cut taxes by 33 percent)," Neal contends. "It was the wrong way. The Republicans have always favored cutting the budget — that's what the people want — and this is what the Democrats are doing."

The Republican situation is much better in Indiana, Neal says, but again his honesty flows forward.

Listen:

"I think we can nominate (Lt. Gov.) Bob Orr for governor and he would have a good chance to stay in office for eight years .

"I'm sure Doc can beat (Sen. Birch) Bayh. I hope he will run. After all, he was a legislator before an administrator — and wouldn't that be some team, Lugar and Bowen...

"But you see, all of our strength is at the top, from mayors and the courthouses up, even though there are more Democrats in Indiana than Republicans.

"Those 22 people on the state committee have hardly been innovative and imaginative. They need to broaden the party's base, instead of grabbing on to Bowen to save them."

Neal notes that despite Bowen's and Sen. Richard Lugar's strong victories in 1976, the Republicans lost eight Congressional seats and regained just one in last November's election.

"A committee I served on in '76 recommended better candidate recruitment, but not much happened," he says. "We need some scuba divers to dig out and cultivate candidates, qualified people with broad vision who aren't limited in their perspective and who understand politics. The Democrats have done a better job. I think Bruce Melchert (current state chairman) understands this and will make a good chairman because he will try to broaden the party."

When Neal's not talking politics, he's usually talking newspapers — often about press freedom. Neal, whose grandfather bought the *Ledger* in 1914, made national headlines in July 1965, when he got into a free press battle with Hamilton Circuit Court Judge Edward New, Jr.

After New decreed a tough policy on moving traffic violations —

first offenders faced six months at the penal farm — Neal in his front-page column wrote: "This latest edict ... is an excellent example of shotgun justice. ... It isn't necessary to upset a whole community to get at the handful of motorists who run wild on the highways."

New promptly cited Neal for criminal contempt, saying he "published and distributed ...a disdainful, despicable, scurrilous and contemptuous article about this court ...."

Time magazine, newspapers ranging from the *New York Times* to the *Brazil* (Ind.) *Times*, and electronic media reported and/or commented on the case.

Neal was released on $50,000 bond — and eventually, after dragging on for more than 18 months, the case was dismissed in Hancock County.

Neal thinks Indiana's Open Door Law, passed by the 1977 General Assembly, "will be picked at, and we will have to keep going back each year (to protect it)."

Although he thinks "things will get worse between the media and the bar," he feels good about how his community's officials have accepted the new law.

And it's Noblesville and Hamilton County where things count the most with Neal.

"In Noblesville I'm a liberal," he says. "Where we can see our problems and know what we're doing with our money — for the elderly, say — I'm liberal.

"But when it comes to Indianapolis and Indiana politics, I'm ultraconservative, because I don't think money is going to the right places."

He's asked one final question: If the Republicans began squabbling anew and Otis Bowen called on him, would he serve again?

"No," he replies. "I had my turn. It's the only thing I wouldn't do for the governor."

And so Jim Neal will remain Jim Neal — a newspaper editor who once received much attention for his political medicine but today doesn't get a second glance from a head waiter or hotel manager.

Road to SALT dotted with minefields

Nixon Hoosier Feature Service, March 1979

    Shortly after the Carter Administration took office, it invited newspapers to attend a two-day foreign policy conference. Joe Nixon, president of Nixon Newspapers, urged me to attend. He had a strong interest in foreign policy. The conference at the State Department drew some 300 editors from around the country.
    Among the topics was the SALT II agreement. I wrote this story and three others for the Nixon Hoosier Feature Service.

WASHINGTON — For sale: one SALT II Treaty.

Seller: The Carter Administration.

Hoped-for buyer: The United States Senate.

Appearing late last month at a State Department foreign policy conference, government spokesmen didn't sound like carnival hawkers, but they repeatedly pushed the critical importance of getting a strategic arms treaty signed — and without strings.

A litany of buzz words were orally Xeroxed during two days of meetings: verification, stability, deterrence, equivalency and linkage.

In short, SALT II can be compared to professional football strategy: defense –deterrence — is the name of the game.

Paul Warnke, former director of the U.S. Arms Control and Disarmament Agency, noted SALT has just one objective: to improve the United States' security by making nuclear war less likely.

Warnke, who has been pictured as too dovish in his dealings with the Russians, explained that SALT allows only new weapons or improvement of strategic balance. At the same time, the agreement moves toward ending development of "destabilizing" — offensive —

weapons.

SALT II, which would remain in force until 1985, would initially limit each nation to a total of 2,400 strategic nuclear delivery vehicles, with a reduction to 2,250 planned "well before 1985."

Despite the reductions — for the first time in the nuclear arms race — the agreement allows the United States to develop the cruise missile for placement on heavy, strategic bombers.

Like the Trident submarines, which have great range but are immune from Soviet attack, the cruise missile is not a first-strike weapon, intended as an attacking instrument.

Which raises the question of second-strike capability.

Asked to respond to Senate Minority Leader Howard Baker's view that the U.S. can't be certain of its ability to obliterate the Soviets' second-strike system, Warnke's answer was flip: "We can do much more damage to the Soviets on our first strike than they can to us, so I would advise Sen. Baker to worry about something else."

Warnke doesn't have to deal with Sen. Baker, a likely Republican presidential candidate and key Senate figure. Brian Atwood, deputy assistant secretary for congressional relations in the State Department, does.

Atwood followed Warnke to the podium and, while admitting there is strong opposition to SALT Il, insisted there is a distinction between opposition and criticism. He noted that while Sen. Henry Jackson, long recognized as a weapons expert, has criticized the agreement he has not announced his opposition.

Asked if credibility is a problem in light of recent events involving Russia and the U.S., Atwood said there can't be another missile debate in the country, "because too much information is available."

That wealth of information is welcomed, he said, because it will define what is "really in our best interests," and thus will eliminate the credibility problem.

Which leads to the question of verification.

Warnke, Carter's key negotiator before returning to his private law practice, answered by saying he was "satisfied with verification provisions, because they're ours in SALT I ... and they're not as complex in SALT II."

He said Russia has accepted a prohibition on using equipment that would jam signals needed for intelligence.

Atwood said that once either side begins testing, the other side knows to some degree what is taking place.

He cited the Poseidon missile as an example. If a strategic arms planner asked a weapons engineer if a 15th warhead could be added to the 14 in place, the answer would be yes. But testing would be required to make sure the first 14 still work properly — and thus verification would not be difficult for the Soviets.

In the final analysis, the treaty comes down to making each side equivalent in nuclear strength, with no "winners" and "losers," a matter of strategic parity, with neither side having an advantage of striking first.

The consequences of treaty failure are enormous, Warnke, Atwood and others insist. They argue that Soviet relations will worsen, that Russia will not get out of Africa and that, in general, "local competitions" will only be exacerbated.

Which raises the question of "linkage."

The Carter administration argues that linking SALT to other problems — Iran, Southeast Asia, China-Soviet relations — is wrong, that the treaty question must stand alone.

"Our strategy is to take the high ground," Atwood said. "We welcome debate."

Warnke, perhaps trying to shake his soft image, didn't sound like he was on high ground when asked about linkage.

"A narrow concept," he asserted. "An absurdity. Obviously we would not sign a treaty that was not in our best interests."

But then he backed off slightly when he said the treaty should be considered in the "overall situation." He noted President Johnson postponed SALT discussions in 1968 when the Soviets invaded Czechoslavakia.

One thing is for sure: No matter the outcome, defense spending will not decrease. Warnke says failure to get SALT II will mean a budget increase of $5 to $7 billion a year for a few years, with an additional $100 billion for development of new systems. An agreement will mean more spending, but not nearly as great.

The Senate debate will begin soon. There are reports that the administration has only 40 of 67 votes needed, with another 20 undecided.

It will be a tough selling job for Atwood and his cohorts — but unlike the Panama Canal treaties, polls show that more than 80 percent of the American public favors signing the SALT II treaty.

Ruckelshaus: We're still suffering from Watergate

Newspapers, August 1979

In October 1973, Indiana native William Ruckelshaus became part of the "Saturday Night Massacre."

After leaving government service, Ruckelshaus joined Weyerhaeuser Corporation, which produces paper products, in Federal Way, Washington.

I caught up with him the last week of July 1979 for a retrospective look at his career at the Environmental Protection Agency and, of course, that exercise of raw political power some six years earlier.

I interrupted a vacation in Los Angeles for a one-day trip to Federal Way, where Ruckelshaus and I had lunch in a Weyerhaeuser dining room that looked out over gorgeous Pacific Northwest scenery.

My long, taped interview resulted in four stories — two major pieces and two sidebars.

FEDERAL WAY, Wash. — As autumn's leaves died that Oct. 20 in Washington, D.C., William D. Ruckelshaus knew his government career was dying, too.

Saddened, deeply disappointed, he strolled from the office of his boss, Attorney General Elliot L. Richardson, to his own Justice Department office.

It was 6 p.m. on a Saturday, and Richardson had just told former Hoosier Ruckelshaus that he had resigned after refusing President Richard Nixon's order to fire Watergate Special Prosecutor Archibald Cox.

Now, summoned to answer a telephone call from Nixon's chief aide, Gen. Alexander Haig, Ruckelshaus knew that he, too, after refusing to fire Cox, would be forced to resign as deputy attorney general.

That was in 1973, and that day would become known as the "Saturday Night Massacre," leaving Richardson, Ruckelshaus and Cox victims of a political scandal that Ruckelshaus believes remains imbedded in the nation's heart.

"I think the consequences of Watergate are enormous," the 47-year-old Ruckelshaus says, shifting his lanky 6-2 frame. He is sitting in the fifth-floor executive dining room of Weyerhaeuser Corporation, of which he became senior vice president for legal and corporate affairs in 1976 after practicing law in D.C. for three years.

"I think we've got a serious, deepening—hopefully, not permanent—erosion of trust in our basic institutions and leadership," he continues, looking through a floor-to ceiling glass wall that allows a postcard view of the Pacific Northwest: sunshine piercing a flat blue sky, Mt. Rainier rising in the distance, giant evergreens protecting placid maples, and a man-made, 10-acre lake directly below housing rainbow trout, swans and Canada honkers.

Ruckelshaus, named by President Nixon as the Environmental Protection Agency's first administrator in 1970, cites three critical E's to support his view that a lack of trust stemming from Watergate compounds the nation's difficulties today.

"We let problems like the environment, our economy, energy and the interrelationship between the last two sit on the back burner for more than two years without the President focusing toward some solutions in the public interest," he says. "The only issue was (the President's survival), and all these problems were swept aside. We are suffering today dearly."

Republican Ruckelshaus, whose comments came six days before Democrat Jimmy Carter told the nation it is suffering from a "crisis of confidence," doesn't think Watergate initiated the erosion of trust. Nor, he says, has Watergate, alone, caused the continued slippage.

He asserts that Carter, himself, has contributed to his inability to solve the energy problem "by jumping all over the big oil companies."

Ruckelshaus pauses, digs into rolled roast beef and cottage cheese, then: "We're looking for villains everywhere, we're looking for conspiracies everywhere. As a result, we're not dealing with the basics involved in energy, and I think it is at least partially a result of this enormous erosion."

Despite his strong views about Watergate's damaging aftermath, Ruckelshaus disagrees with Judge John Sirica, who in a new book says he wishes President Nixon had been tried.

A trial would have continued to force the country's attention on problems "not central to its survival," Ruckelshaus contends. "I don't see anything that would have been gained."

Ruckelshaus feels that even today, the country is still not focusing with sufficient intensity and understanding on survival problems — energy, economy, world interdependence, burgeoning population in relationship to diminishing resources.

Although deeply disappointed that night in 1973 — he was convinced it was wrong to fire Cox, who was doing his job by subpoening the Watergate tapes — Ruckelshaus holds no personal rancor toward Nixon.

"I hope he will somehow find peace," he says. "I would hope that he'd sit down there in San Clemente, or wherever, and grow old gracefully and quietly."

And yet, Ruckelshaus, too, is frank in assessing Nixon's motives that led to the mass firing: "All Cox was really trying to do was find out who was involved, and I think he was getting too close to the President. The President wanted to call the whole thing off. This (firing Cox) was his way of doing it. He didn't get away with it."

Did the firing change Ruckelshaus as a person?

"Oh, yes, sure," he responds quickly. "I had, after all, spent six years in that administration, working very hard toward what I thought was a series of policies in the public interest. And then to have the President reveal himself as he did in the transcripts, as somebody not worthy of the kind of support that I had given him, was very disappointing. I left feeling very sad.

"It didn't lessen my interest or enthusiasm for government, but it certainly gave me a tremendous feeling of loss, considering the opportunities the President had, after being elected in 1972 with an overwhelming majority, to do something about the country's problems."

When asked, Ruckelshaus admits he might have been naive to the extent that he suffered from supporting Nixon "with so much fervor. I disillusioned myself into believing Nixon was something that he turned out not to be."

He thinks his Hoosier background might have contributed to his naivete: "I think there is a tradition in Indiana of straightforwardness, directness that is not seen everywhere."

Does that mean the Indianapolis-born Ruckelshaus might return someday to Hoosier politics?

That's highly unlikely; politics would only be incidental to what he was doing as a private citizen, should he return, he replies. He's not interested in being governor. And where he once wanted very much to be senator — Birch Bayh beat back his challenge in 1967 — the U.S. Senate no longer interests him.

After having gone through the pain of Watergate—and apparently surviving it quite well — it's easy to see how Ruckelshaus feels about politics, as he digs into cantaloupe with mint ice cream and breathes in the beauty surrounding him.

Lugar tells executives he wants to hold SALT aces

Nixon Newspapers, Dec. 12, 1979

When an aide to Republican Senator Richard Lugar called me and asked if Nixon Newspapers executives would like to have a private dinner with the senator, I said yes. NNI president Joe Nixon suggested that his wife, Marian (a Republican; Joe was a Democrat), prepare a meal at the Nixon home.

It was a fascinating evening that included four NNI executives and their wives and John Nixon's oldest son, Greg. It was no gabfest. Lugar spoke frankly, and what he said made news.

I wrote the following piece, which resulted in a note from Lugar that said in part: "I have read your lengthy article drawn from our discussion of several days ago, and found it accurate in every respect. Congratulations on a well-written piece."

Praise is nice, but what I really treasure is Lugar saying that the news story, which involved a complex subject, was "accurate in every respect."

Richard Lugar wants to play out the United States' hand in the biggest pot thus far in what be calls a "cosmic poker game" with the Soviet Union.

As an historic vote on the Strategic Arms Limitation Treaty — SALT II — draws closer, Lugar remains opposed, preferring to gamble that the Russians will agree to reopen negotiations that could lead to a stronger United States hand.

He discussed his position Saturday night at dinner with four Nixon Newspapers Inc. executives and their wives in the Wabash home of NNI Vice President Joe Nixon.

"You have to assume, as a treaty opponent, that the administration might be right about the Soviet Union refusing to go back to the negotiating table," Lugar, Indiana's Republican junior senator, said.

"Are you willing to take the risk?" the proponents ask.

Lugar's willing. He thinks he and others have a good bet that the Soviet Union will reopen bargaining because the Russians also face serious risks if SALT fails. One Soviet fear, he said, is the United States' proven technological inventiveness that could proceed unhampered without the treaty.

Sitting across from a crackling fireplace, Lugar sipped post-dinner coffee and said his gamble also is based in part on conversations be and other senators had this summer with Russian Premier Aleksei Kosygin.

The talks played a part in Lugar's primary reason for opposing SALT—that the United States is not provided with absolute verification measures.

A member of the Senate Foreign Relations committee, Lugar saw one of his verification amendments fall last week as the committee, on Friday, approved SALT by a 9-6 vote.

Denying the measure was a "killer" amendment — the kind that, if approved, would force the Russians to reject the treaty — Lugar told the small gathering he wants "absolute verification procedures," adding:

"We depended on the Iranian sites for telemetry (radio signals from space) and now these are gone. The Turks stopped us when we wanted to use U-2s to fly over mountain ranges."

Lugar said that when he suggested on-site inspection for both sides in his conversation with Kosygin, the Russian leader replied: "We think we know enough of what we need to know," indicating the Soviet Union may feel it has the strongest position on verification.

Echoing the arguments of another foreign relations committee member, Ohio Democrat John Glenn, Lugar said telemetry is crucial, because it provides much more than photographic intelligence.

"Telemetry can tell us about different characteristics, such as speed, that photography won't," he said. "If the Soviet Union sends telemetry in different wavelengths than we're prepared to intercept, we've had it. We've argued that telemetry should not be denied us. Up to 18 months ago, both sides even denied using telemetry (because of its strategic importance)."

Lugar again asserted that the treaty doesn't provide for true reductions in nuclear weapons, saying: "The proponents' only case is that if you vote for this treaty (which would be in effect until 1985), you would at least preserve the nuclear reduction process."

Asked how he thought the vote would go today, he said the administration can now count on 50 of 67 votes needed, with 30 senators opposing and the other 20 uncommitted.

Political consideration will play a crucial role, he said. "Some people think they gave their word too soon on the Panama Canal from the standpoint of a quid pro quo, so they will stay undecided for a longer time," Lugar explained.

He thinks the administration might try a few test votes, such as on the Backfire bomber issue — there is debate over its importance to the Soviet arsenal — after the Thanksgiving holiday.

Tying in SALT with defense spending, Lugar said: "The treaty initially was sold as an economy move. I've come to the conclusion that it won't be. ...

"There is no evidence that the Soviet Union is prepared to stop spending 15 percent more each year on defense, and thus we have to spend more to keep up. We're losing influence with our allies, and SALT has brought this to the fore."

Saying he favors a 5 percent increase in defense spending — others argue for 3 percent — Lugar expressed sympathy for President Carter on this issue:

"He has a real political problem. He has Democrats Henry Jackson (Wash.) and Sam Nunn (Ga.) arguing for more defense and George McGovern (S.D.) and William Proxmire (Wisc.) saying the price is too high. Carter is trying to weave through it bit by bit, and the fact that the defense budget is going to Congress two months in advance is unprecedented."

That Carter political problem led to the question of who Lugar thinks will get the Democratic presidential nomination, Carter or Edward Kennedy.

"Kennedy will be the nominee, I think," Lugar responded. "I think the country would be safer with Carter than Kennedy. I think Kennedy will win the big states, but I think Carter could hang on a long time (in the convention balloting)."

Lugar, of course, is deeply involved in the Republican race, acting as campaign manager for Senate Minority Leader Howard Baker (Tenn.), who, Lugar said, agrees with his view that the Soviets will return to the negotiating table before letting SALT die.

Lugar said he chose Baker because he thinks the Tennessean has the best chance "to put together coalitions that can bring changes. He's a consummate politician."

Is Lugar a vice-president possibility?

The answer was a quick, convincing no. In fact, Lugar revealed, for the first time, that he's part of a select group now choosing a Baker running mate.

Lugar would not reveal who the possibilities are, but said the list has been narrowed to less than five. He said Baker hopes to announce the choice before the New Hampshire primary in January.

And Baker's chances?

Lugar readily conceded that Ronald Reagan is the frontrunner, but sounded confident as he discussed "ifs" and "buts" and "likelies" that could result in Baker being the ultimate compromise choice when the Grand Old Party gathers in Detroit next summer to choose its nominee.

Professor wary of warlike mood

Nixon Hoosier Feature Service, February 1980

Little Manchester College in northern Wabash County, Ind., had carved out quite a reputation for its peace program, so I decided to interview Professor Ken Brown, an introspective, charismatic academic. The piece distributed by the feature service got wide play, including a big spread in the Sunday edition of a newspaper in upstate New York.

NORTH MANCHESTER — His name is Ken Brown, and most Americans today would probably dismiss him as a naive academician from a little backwater school in a sleepy Indiana burg of 5,000 folks.

But when the subject is peace, it's hard to ignore Manchester College here, which has one of only six peace studies programs in the nation ("Analysis of War and Peace," "Current Issues in Peace and Justice").

And while philosophy professor Kenneth L. Brown's ideas might sound like an egghead's silly dreams, they emanate from a man who has thought much about and thoroughly studied justice since age 6, when a "playground jury" falsely convicted him of pushing another youngster off a slide.

A soft-spoken, bookish man of 46 who epitomizes the peace dove, Brown displays a war hawk's toughness advocating his views in the face of America's growing anger as Russia squats in Afghanistan and Iran shackles 50 Yanks.

Brown, who earned his Ph.D. at Duke University, stakes out this position: World peace could be achieved without militaristic bloodshed if leaders abandoned long-held — and, in his view, false — assumptions.

Claiming that "our social and moral thinking lags behind our technological thinking," Brown ticks off the assumptions:

— Military power protects wealth, and, at the same time, produces prosperity.

— Preparation for war is the best preparation for peace. If we have a strong military, we won't use it.

— A balance of power in the United States' favor against Russia leads to and preserves peace.

— Winning the arms race makes the U.S. more secure. Military power is essential for America because it's a matter of choosing between freedom or slavery and Christianity or godless atheism.

A lot of bunk, Brown says, leaning back in a chair inside an office nook decorated in wall-to-wall books.

Knowing that he's part of just 8 percent that says the nation should spend less on defense (according to a recent poll), Brown attacks the assumptions with professorial empiricism.

He chides those who say "a little-war is good for the economy," and he turns to Kenneth E. Boulding, a Colorado economics professor, for support.

Boulding, in his 1978 book, *Stable Peace*, claims that wealth creates power and power destroys wealth. Brown reads from Boulding's book:

"Indeed, in terms of economic development in the 20th Century, it has been the losers in war who have been the principle gainers and the winners who have been the losers; Japan and Germany are prize examples."

Removing his glasses and looking up, Brown says the Depression taught America a wrong lesson: "We primed the pump to get us out of the Depression, and it helped in the short range. But in the long range, high military spending depletes capital and hurts our science and research community.

"We've fallen behind in everything from 'K-Mart'... cameras to cars, because 40 percent of our laboratory scientists have been siphoned off for military research."

Turning to another assumption, Brown insists that Congressman Floyd Fithian, who serves North Manchester, and others are wrong when they say preparation for war is the best preparation for peace.

"Studies show that the opposite is true." Brown says. "When you prepare for war you get it. If we create a ready deployment force, as the Administration is now talking about, we'll wind up using it."

Countering those who claim winning the arms race is vital to America's security, Brown contends that the arms race in itself breeds insecurity.

Tying that argument in with the balance of power assumption, he claims that "attempts at balance don't work, so we end up with an arms race."

Brown, who specializes in American religious thought and political philosophy, moves to another point — the freedom or slavery assumption. He argues that the United States has "involved itself with tyrants, fascists and terrorists, all in the name of 'freedom', and muddied the picture."

Names roll off his tongue like tanks advancing into battle: Somoza, Diem, Allende, Park, the shah…

The word "slavery" diverts Brown to his basic premise: false assumptions. He sharpens his position:

"Our basic assumptions about war and peace are the same as the assumptions people made for centuries for slavery and divine right of kings. People thought social order would be destroyed without them, that a state church was needed to politically enforce morality. We've overcome those assumptions.

"As long as world society does not challenge today's assumptions, nothing will happen."

The author of several articles on peace for religion publications, Brown chastises the Christianity or godless atheism assumption: "It's not that simple. Most of our fighting has been for our pocketbook, not for God. Both cultures tend to be materialistic. Ours is much more politically humane, but beware when we fight a monster lest we become a monster.

"If we are Christian, our actions must be different. Our behavior different. Labels are cheap.

"We need to make a shift in which the foundation for our patriotism and our national pride is our morality.…Washington, Lincoln, Puritans, the Peace Corps. Not in brutality.

"We haven't been able to grasp, embrace and practice moral truths."

But in the final analysis, can the Russians be trusted? Brown is asked.

"Obviously, no, when it comes to the super powers, and that's the problem," he admits, sliding into a defensive posture:

"Fundamental morality escapes nation states. But we have to ask ourselves how do we develop viable human relationships that lead to peace. You do so by willing to risk trusting."

Risk trusting the Russians?

"It will fail less than where we're headed now, which is a spiral of action and reaction," he says calmly.

Does that mean World War III is near?

"I'm not sure," Brown says: "All I know is the mood is bad."

Which leads to Afghanistan. Brown thinks that conflict "will cost the Soviets tremendously," that "the Russians have made almost as big a blunder as the United States did supporting Vietnam's puppet regimes."

The worst thing the United States can now do is to imitate the Russians in the Middle East, he says, adding:

"We need to learn new ways to resist evil ... we need to get rid of the false ready deployment assumption."

Even if those assumptions were destroyed, could true world peace ever be achieved?

"No, not the absence of conflict," he responds. "Yes, if you're talking about organized, large-scale, systematic destruction."

You sound like a "bleeding heart," Brown is told.

He smiles, puts his right hand under his heart, protected by a white dress shirt and brown high-neck sweater.

"We need more bleeding hearts," he says. "We need a renewed sense of reverence for life."

Willkie's steamy return to Elwood

Nixon Hoosier Feature Service, August 1980

This is an "anniversary" piece that recalls a great moment in Indiana — nay, American — history.

ELWOOD — They swallowed up the town.

They formed rivers of humanity that flowed to Callaway Park, where, 250,000 strong, they smothered the park's 40.6 acres.

They came in 103-degree heat to see a man whose charisma was penetrating the nation in a time of despair.

That was 40 years ago tomorrow, in another presidential year, when Wendell Willkie returned here — his hometown of 10,000 people — to formally accept the Republican presidential nomination.

Bernard Schuck was there. George Stout, Richard Dellinger and Charles Windsor were there. And they still remember.

Oh, was Charles Windsor there! He was up there on the huge wooden platform that accommodated 1,000 dignitaries.

Opposite the platform were 30,000 chairs that kept Windsor awake one night as he figured out how to arrange them so everyone could see and still leave aisles for safety.

Windsor was a 33-year-old, self-employed civil engineer who had been assigned to organize what he now calls "an American phenomenon."

Hyperbole? Maybe.

But here was Willkie — a true "people's choice" — overcoming frontrunners Thomas Dewey of New York, Sen. Robert Taft of Ohio and Sen. Arthur Vandenburg of Michigan to score a sixth-ballot victory in metropolitan Philadelphia and choosing to accept the nomination in grassroots Elwood.

Here was Willkie, once an avowed Democrat, grabbing the highest Republican honor, despite not having a real political base, and opting for his hometown, where many people had forgotten all about him over the years.

And here was Elwood, suddenly faced with preparing — in three weeks — for a major American event that would involve more than a quarter of a million people.

The country's mood also played a major role in the "phenomenon," said Windsor, now an active, 73-year-old history buff.

"There was worry and desperation about the economy, even though more people were working," he explained as he walked with a visitor through Callaway Park. "People felt broke all the time. And the country was heading for war with Germany and Italy.

"The Republicans were really down in the mouth ... for eight years under (President Franklin D.) Roosevelt. Then along came this very engaging man of great vigor."

An Anderson, Ind., native, Windsor had been home a short time after working for the federal government on projects in the South when he was approached by Harry Hudson, Madison County's Republican chairman.

"Charlie, you've got to organize this thing," he told Windsor.

At first, expectations were relatively small — about 100,000 people witnessing Willkie's speech from the steps of the high school building, above which still stand these words: The Hope of Our Country.

But Mayor George M. Bonham — one of only three Republicans ever to hold the office in heavily Democratic Elwood — quickly realized the event was ballooning. Fast.

The owner of Elwood's only hotel, Bonham, as mayor, received a Western Union wire from the chairman of a California delegation. It read: "Reserve us 50 rooms in your best hotel." Bonham's quiet little place had 28 rooms.

Meanwhile, a local Republican committee asked farmer-businessman Homer Capehart, later elected to the U.S. Senate, to be general chairman.

A year earlier, Capehart had received favorable recognition after hosting a "Cornfield Conference" of Republican leaders at his Washington, Ind., farm.

Windsor had the toughest task. For starters, he and Tipton County surveyor Lou Richards had to build two 54-foot temporary bridges across Duck Creek, which circles Callaway Park to the east and south. The bridges were necessary to get heavy trucks, filled with chairs, lumber and other supplies, into the park on Elwood's northeast side.

And then there was the matter of cars. Windsor and a parking committee planned for at least 30,000 by contracting for 350 acres north and east of the park. Four hundred people were hired to direct traffic.

Deeply concerned about safety, Windsor arranged for crews to pick up thousands of small stones that lined pathways through Callaway. Roots that stuck up over the ground were yanked and hauled away. There would be no broken ankles or cut legs as people forged into the park, Windsor hoped.

There'd be no thirsts left unquenched either. Windsor installed water lines for additional drinking fountains that would be needed on a hot summer's day.

Still, to guard against heat prostration, Red Cross emergency tents were planned. Good thing. Several people collapsed that sun-drenched Aug. 17.

Another major task was installing wiring and telephone lines needed to carry Willkie's message. Amplifiers were positioned to carry the speech more than a square mile in the park. And, in those non-television days, telephones and sending equipment were needed for the huge press corps.

Finally, the chairs.

"A call went out to every funeral home in central Indiana," Windsor said with a smile. "I spent one night lying in bed laying out the seating arrangement. We laid out the chairs with string, held in place with nails in the grass, so the workers knew where to put all the seats."

Caught up in the hoopla and pride — Willkie is the only native

Hoosier to be nominated for President — the Democrat-controlled county commissioners helped out. They assigned crews to oil dusty roads. Democrat Gov. Clifford Townsend followed along, offering the Indiana State Police's services.

The result was "like a tremendous picnic celebration," Windsor said. "There were no fights. Everybody was good-natured."

Almost everybody.

Concessionaires who expected to rake in money at a time when the country was still feeling the Great Depression struggled to break even. Grocery stores, which had stocked up heavily on food items, also suffered.

"People weren't used to buying (prepared) food," Windsor said. "Some brought picnic lunches, but most people wanted something to drink."

The hamburger hustlers, mostly homeowners who set up stands on their property near the park, got stung. So did Dietzen Bakery.

Bernard Schuck recalls with a laugh: "Drew Pearson wrote a column about it. He said the only guy who made money was a farmer named Tony Schafer. Dietzen called him up and said he could have all the leftover buns if he hauled them away. He did and fed them to his hogs."

Leftover buns, indeed. Pearson reported that when Dietzen asked Capehart, an expansive, outgoing man, whether 1,000 buns would be enough, Capehart boomed: "A thousand!? This, thing is going to be big. Make it 10,000!"

But from the very beginning, people mostly sought liquid refreshment.

The visiting thousands who had arrived the night before crowded into the taverns, where air-conditioning — rare in those days — cooled them. Then they went to cars to sleep off their stupor.

Mountains of beer cans filled the streets. Runnels of brew flowed through downtown alleys.

Schuck — a staunch Democrat — did not see Willkie speak; instead he was directing traffic at 28th Street on the east edge of town.

Some of the 40,000 persons who had come by train from several states marched by him.

"You could get a round-trip train ride out of Pennsylvania and a box lunch for $5," Schuck said. "They dropped people off at a siding a couple of miles out of town and they walked in."

Some people never reached the park. Schuck remembered the man who walked against the mob heading for Callaway: "I said to him, 'Why are you going this way?' He said, 'It's hot and dusty and I've got 12 cans of cold beer and a radio in the car.' He was from Philadelphia."

When those heading for the park got thirsty, they found Elwood residents providing ice water — for 15 cents a glass.

George Stout's thirst problem developed after he got into the park.

Now 72, Stout recalled: "I was supposed to go home, but I got mixed in with the crowd and drifted to the park. My wife and child were waiting for me. I got the dickens for not returning home.

"When I got to the park, I climbed up on a beam that was supporting a press stand. I stayed up there for about three hours because I was afraid of losing my place. I was very thirsty, but I saw history being made before me."

What Stout also saw was humanity packed as far as his eyes could see, topped by a dust cloud that resembled a weather inversion.

What kind of man was this Willkie, who could magnetize 250,000 people to a small Indiana town in the rather dark days of 1940?

Richard Dellinger, who was 4 years old that day and remembers seeing "a lot of knees," provides one answer.

Now a state representative and history/social studies teacher in Noblesville, Dellinger says:

"He was news. He was a non-politician who dared to speak his criticism of big government and the New Deal policies of Roosevelt.

"FDR was finishing his second term and was not news. His popularity had declined somewhat with the deeper period of depression in 1936 and his proposed court-packing plan. Willkie was viewed as an alternative."

As an alternative, Willkie had come from practically nowhere. He had not achieved recognition through previous political ventures, but — as Dellinger alluded to — by acting as an attorney representing big business against big government.

In the early 1930s he worked for the Ohio Edison Co., later absorbed by the Commonwealth and Southern Corporation. Willkie eventually succeeded Bernard C. Cobb, who had "discovered" him, as president of the firm, which had assets of more than $1 billion.

Willkie drew attention when he fought the Tennessee Valley Authority during the government's power experiments in Tennessee and Mississippi, the territory of Commonwealth and Southern.

At the time, most businessmen supported not fighting government regulation until public opinion was more favorable to business.

Willkie, though, chose to fight—for six years. When the government offered Commonwealth and Southern $67,000,000 for its Tennessee Electric Power holdings, Willkie insisted on $90,000,000. The government and the company compromised on $78,600,000, prompting Willkie to remark, "That's a lot of money for an Indiana farmer to be kicking around."

Willkie was no farmer. He and his four brothers and two sisters grew up as children of attorneys; his mother was the first Madison County woman to pass the bar.

Four years before Wendell was born in 1892, his family moved to Elwood from Lagro, Ind., where Herman Willkie was school superintendent. He took the same position in Elwood while he finished reading for the law.

Like his siblings, Wendell developed a sharp mind, enhanced by his parents' private library. He was graduated from Indiana University Law School and returned to Elwood to practice with his father.

Willkie enlisted when World War I broke out. Until then, he had gone by his given name: Lewis Wendell Willkie. But a clerk had erred in recording his name, making it Wendell Lewis Willkie — and Willkie kept it that way.

After being discharged, Willkie returned to Elwood, but, faced with the difficult task of rebuilding his law practice, accepted a position with Firestone Tire and Rubber Co. in Akron, Ohio.

Commonwealth and Southern, based in New York, came next. Corporate law fascinated Willkie, but his future — politics — was ahead of him. He was a natural, what with his striking build — slightly more than 6 feet — handsomeness, law background and Indiana University debate team experience.

Dellinger terms Willkie's amateur effort at achieving the Republican nomination as "probably the single most successful grassroots movement in our time.

"The convention itself was manipulated by the amateurs and some young pros — Congressman Charlie Halleck of Indiana among them — to get the nomination for Willkie. The galleries were packed with Willkie supporters who chanted, 'We want Willkie' at the slightest provocation."

But Willkie's political future would end quickly, suddenly. After losing to Roosevelt, Willkie in 1942 became FDR's personal representative in an overseas tour of Allied nations. Out of his travels came his book, "One World," which drew critical acclaim.

On Oct. 7, 1944, Willkie died unexpectedly. He was gone, but his life — and that day in August, 1940 — were left imprinted in the annals of American political history.

English professor wages battle on censorship

Nixon Hoosier Feature Service, May 1981

This piece was intended to run only in the Nixon papers, but it received such a strong reaction, we syndicated it and it ran in several papers, including the Chicago Tribune.

BLOOMINGTON—He has been called a communist, smut peddler and corrupter of youth.

He has popped up on television screens, spoken before countless audiences and written one book and numerous articles in a battle he has waged for 10 years: to free the minds of young people so they can have thoughts of their own.

It is a battle that he and others feel they must win to prevent a growing, dangerous menace in America: censorship of books in school libraries and classrooms.

His name is Edward Jenkinson, and he simply wants to be known as a concerned parent of three children ranging in age from 28 months to 21 years.

An Indiana University English professor, Jenkinson sits in his office at the English Curriculum Study Center, of which he is director, and talks almost non-stop about mind control, parents' obligations and worst cases of school censorship.

"I am first and foremost a parent — that's where I came to this issue," he says in a soft, velvety voice. "When did it say when I got my bachelor degree and became a teacher I would automatically be sterilized?"

While working as an English curriculum director 10 years ago at I.U., Jenkinson's intrigue with that censorship question mounted as it continually arose.

Jenkinson recalls the recent Warsaw controversy, in which a school board member told the *Indianapolis News* that in the final analysis, it's a matter of who will control young people's minds.

"My concern is not who will control minds, but who will free minds," he says. "I want my kids, your kids, everybody's kids in the country to grow up free to read, free to ask questions, free to challenge, and, above all, free to have thoughts of their own.

"And I pray that kids will have knowledge and understanding to ask those questions intelligently, to form responsible challenges and have thoughts that will keep them free."

Jenkinson staunchly defends the rights of parents to be concerned, complain about books and ask for alternate assignments if they feel their children are being asked to read something that's harmful.

"But I don't think that gives me the right, as a parent, to say that anybody in my daughter's class, school, county, state or nation can't read a particular book," he adds, his voice rising slightly as he removes thick-lensed glasses and leans back in his chair.

The conversation is interrupted briefly when Jenkinson is called out of his office to meet with a student. It gives the visitor an opportunity to glance around. Books everywhere — from Herman Melville's *Moby Dick* to Col. Robert L. Scott's *God is My Co-Pilot*. Later, the visitor learns that Jenkinson has 6,000 books at the curriculum center and another 4,000 books at home.

Back from meeting with the student, Jenkinson returns to his straight-back utility chair, puts a hand to thinning hair and doesn't miss a beat:

"We parents who object to a book have an obligation and responsibility to read it first. The worst kind of censorship incidents are when people act unilaterally to get rid of things in schools without ever having read them."

He cites the case of an Indiana high school principal who received a call from a parent objecting to his child being assigned to read Arthur

Miller's *Death of a Salesman*. The principal promised he would get rid of that "novel."

Jenkinson tosses out two more cases, one in which a school board member objected to *Making It With Madamoiselle* and another in which *Belly Button Defense* ran into trouble.

In the "Mademoiselle" case, a school board member was embarrassed to learn that the book contained dress patterns. *Belly Button Defense* is about basketball.

Jenkinson asserts: "There are parents who don't want their children exposed to any realities of life in the schools. That's their privilege, but it doesn't extend to the other students.

"These realities coincide with the parents' knowledge of the world, their political, religious, social, economic, moral perspectives.

"It's incumbent that people making charges to find out what's actually being taught before complaining. Such as in sex education courses. Since when has depiction of the human body become pornographic? I'm talking about figures you find in a biology book, reproductions of work by great artists.

"Where would we be if we allowed a wholesale cleaning of our libraries? I think we should teach people how to read, rather than to encourage them to ban books they don't like."

In a speech given April 11 at Ball State University, where Jenkinson got his bachelor's degree in journalism, he expounded on that point:

"I do not pick up a book expecting it to reinforce my own biases, my own knowledge, my own feelings. I do not expect an author to write every word so that it will match my own political, religious, social and economic points of view. Rather, I approach a book expecting to find new information, different points of view, different perspectives."

Jenkinson thinks censorship has increased, in part, because groups such as the Moral Majority interpreted the Republicans' recent victories as "a mandate to go out and 'clean up' the nation's schools." "Clean up" strikes fear in people, indicates something is wrong.

"To the best of my knowledge, no court case involving material used in public schools has ever resulted in a decision that material objected to was obscene or pornographic."

Asked what he considers the worst cases of censorship, Jenkinson cites three:

• Warsaw — the worst case of school censorship — where the school board eliminated books dealing with courses that concerned them.

• Kanawha County, W. Va. — the worst case of violence — where the 1974 textbook war erupted over the total English curriculum adoption for grades 1 through 12. School buses were struck by sniper fire, schools were firebombed and coal miners went on strike.

• Anaheim, Calif. — the worst case of academic freedom — where teachers were told to compile a list of their favorite books. The school board then issued a list, minus some of the teachers' favorites, and told the teachers they could use only the books listed.

Jenkinson can't resist mentioning what he considers one of the most bizarre cases — last January in Omaha. A minister/principal at a private boarding school gathered students and set fire to a pile of books that included "Daffy Duck" comics and National Geographic magazines, saying the books hindered Christian morals.

The Omaha case and a recent incident in Montello, Wisc., are only two in an increasing number.

Judith Krug, director of the Office of Intellectual Freedom for the American Library Association, recently told Jenkinson that censorship has increased five fold since the November 1980 election. At that time, about 300 cases had been reported for each year from 1977 through 1980.

"These are only reported cases," Jenkinson stresses. "It's difficult to get accurate information, because many people don't want to say they have been censored and many school systems don't want that information out. For every Montello, I'd estimate there are another 25 unreported cases."

Earlier this year in Montello, a group of nine parents entered two school libraries, checked out 33 books — some duplicate copies — and were going to keep them, Jenkinson reported. Others in the community convinced the group to return the books.

Included in the Montello seizure were *The Great Gatsby, The Diary of Anne Frank*, and *Catcher in the Rye*. They are all on the top 20 list of most-often banned books, Jenkinson noted. "Catcher" is first.

Says Jenkinson: "*1984* is second, and if that isn't a grand irony. Also taken in Montello was *The Rights of Students*, a paperback published by the American Civil Liberties Union. It's fourth on the top 20."

Jenkinson, whose first book on censorship, *Censors in the Classroom: The Mind Benders* was published in 1979 by the Southern Illinois University Press, is working on another book.

He hopes to get financial support "from somewhere" to study the question full time. He wants to identify the protesting organizations and study the messages they are sending to each other and concerned parents, "because the schools need to know what people are protesting and why."

Jenkinson knows one thing for sure: "Jingoistic replies" from those who fight censorship don't work.

"When educators say things like, 'We're teaching the whole child and not subject matter,' they hurt their cause," he explains. "And when educators don't address the issue and tend to put parents down, they hurt themselves. They say, 'You don't have a college degree, we do.' Big deal."

Jenkinson learned this on one occasion when he appeared on a nationwide television show. A woman from Hattiesburg, Miss., called to take issue, but in the end, Jenkinson and the woman found they agreed on much. What angered the woman, it turned out, was what she felt was the superior attitude of educators.

Meanwhile, Jenkinson gets letters. Nasty ones.

He recently received a letter several pages long, in which the writer accused Jenkinson of being a communist, "because I am a university professor." The writer hurled the other labels, too — smut peddler, corrupter of youth.

"The writer went on for several pages, describing a horrible disease and said he hoped I would contract it," Jenkinson said.

Then a smile wrapped in sadness formed on the professor's beefy, 50-year-old face, and his words tumbled out evenly: "He signed the letter, 'Yours sincerely in Christ.'"

The Battle for Chicago

This is a chapter from *Stuffy: The Life of Newspaper Pioneer Basil "Stuffy" Walters*, published in Spring 1982 by the Iowa State University Press.

The competitive fight in Minneapolis in 1937 shaped up as a citywide brawl when Basil Walters first arrived to direct the *Star*, a dying third, against two solidly entrenched foes. It was different in Chicago in 1944. Walters found a newspaper war zone of much greater depth and intensity.

Foremost among the competitors was Colonel Robert R. McCormick, a "press lord" who insisted he was always right and almost everyone else was wrong. His *Tribune*, which dubbed itself the "World's Greatest Newspaper," had long been the monarch of Chicago journalism. It far outdistanced the field in circulation, but it was losing ground while the others were making gains.

Richard Finnegan, described by contemporaries as a low-keyed man who surprised people with bursts of dynamic action, was quietly building his *Daily Times* in the afternoon field. It was the city's only tabloid. Over at the *Sun*, Marshall Field was receiving high marks as his paper grew, cutting into the *Tribune*'s morning lead.

And then there was Louis Ruppel. An ex-Marine captain, Ruppel was executive editor of William Randolph Hearst's afternoon *Herald American*. He arrived a few weeks after Knight and Walters assumed command at the *Daily News* and immediately let the troops know that a lot of Marine remained in him. He told his people, "What I want around here is a lot of sock! And if I don't get it I'm going to shake you guys up!"

The Chicago newspaper scene was painted in the June 30, 1945, edition of *Collier* magazine. An article entitled "Battle in Printer's Ink," by Herbert Asbury, said, in part:

> Briefly, the editors and publishers of the Windy City are rarin' to go, but because of the newsprint shortage, there is little they can do now except make occasional raids upon rival personnel and plan postwar projects, all of which seem aimed at putting the other fellow out of business. But once wartime restrictions are removed, things should begin to happen.
>
> Almost every newspaperman in Chicago looks for an outbreak of the exciting journalism for which the city has always been famous.
>
> Specifically, they expect a circulation war which may bring nostalgic memories of the bloody battles of more than thirty years ago.

Walters and Knight found Chicago journalism circles bubbling with rumors. Field was going to merge his *Sun* with the *Times*, it was said. He eventually did. Another report said that Hearst, America's number one "press lord," was going to re-enter the morning field. He had earlier closed down his *Examiner*. Others insisted that The Colonel, the number two "press lord" in America, was studying the afternoon field.

McCormick had long fought with his foes, and he wasn't about to back down as World War II came to a close. Early in 1945, the *Tribune* had slipped below a million in circulation for the first time in years, deeply angering the Colonel. And, as Asbury reported, Field had stunned McCormick by stealing Milton Caniff from the Colonel's Tribune-New York News syndicate. Caniff had established himself as one of the country's best comic-strip artists, drawing "Terry and the Pirates," which was being sold to 220 papers at that time. Caniff, however, had to wait until October 1946 to join Field, because he didn't own "Terry" — the Tribune-News syndicate did. It meant he would have to create a new strip. He did. A native of Dayton, where the Wright brothers gave birth to aviation, Caniff came up with air force hero Steve Canyon, which went on to outdo "Terry."

Knight and Walters did not let the rumors, the jockeying for position, the theft of key personnel, and the overall atmosphere distract them from their mission. They were determined to revive the *Daily News* by creating a lively, heavily-local product that featured crisp writing. They wanted to abandon a stodgy, foreign service-dominated product that featured heavy intellectual writing.

That change in direction led to Paul S. Mowrer's resignation as editor three days after Knight took over. It meant the end of a long, dedicated relationship with the *Daily News* that had spanned some forty years.

Mowrer said Knight's editing of the *Daily News* gave him a feeling of desecration. Asbury wrote in *Collier*'s, "Most of the changes in which Mowrer objected were the brain children of Basil (Stuffy) Walters.... Walters is a newspaperman of the dynamic, high-powered school; he believes in flash, a generous use of blackface type, likes an abundance of short, striking human interest stories on page one."

Knight and Walters took the high road to avoid any kind of nastiness with McCormick, Ruppel, or others. When Colonel Knox owned the *Daily News*, the paper responded to McCormick's editorial attacks against it with a series of cartoons portraying McCormick as Colonel McCosmic, a pompous gung-ho, General George Patton-type. Knight ordered the cartoon caricature be dropped. He would win the circulation battle the way he had won others — with unbiased news and staking out the political middle ground between the New Deal-leaning *Times* and *Sun* and the arch-conservative *Tribune* and right-leaning *Herald-American*.

Inside the newsroom, Walters spread praise generously and established a "ping pong" process in which ideas were batted back and forth from Knight to Walters to key editors. Walters encouraged Managing Editor Everett Norlander, City Editor Clem Lane, Foreign Editor Hal O'Flaherty, and News Editor Ed Akers to bounce ideas off each other and himself.

Meanwhile, Walters had been putting together a confidential

notebook of improvements he wanted to introduce one week at a time. He didn't want to do everything at once, "so as not to disturb the solid, though diminishing, core of loyal readers."

Even before arriving in Chicago he knew the paper's news philosophy had to change from an emphasis on foreign service dispatches to much more local news. He felt he was inheriting a good local staff. But he found many reporters were so busy writing books and lecturing, they didn't have enough time to always do a good job for the people who paid them. When he asked a reporter one day why he had not written a good story, the reporter said it was too good for the *Daily News* and that he was saving it for his book.

The foreign staff's dominance discouraged local initiative. One day shortly before Knight's purchase was official, Walters counted only three local stories in the paper. Ed Lahey, who became one of America's great reporters, told Walters jokingly — but bitterly — that the only way to get a local story into the paper was to cable it to Paris and have it cabled back under a Paris dateline.

Less than a month after the purchase, Walters decided to unveil his little strategy notebook to Arthur E. Hall, the *Daily News*' circulation manager.

Hall, told to keep what he saw and heard in the room, bubbled over the planned reforms. He insisted they all be introduced immediately. The situation was so desperate, he argued, the paper couldn't wait for the week-by-week treatment. He revealed that the tabloid *Times* would pass the *Daily News* any day, leaving the *Daily News* fourth in a five-paper field. Said Hall, "The *Times* is cheering every funeral procession by saying, 'There goes another *Daily News* reader.'"

Hall was so convincing, Walters decided to go full throttle and emphasize the new *Daily News* by completely changing it typographically. Histories of the *Daily News* that appeared in the seventies described the changes with mixed views. In the June 1971 edition of the now-deceased *Chicago Journalism Review*, a story appeared entitled "Betraying the Past at the News." It said, in part, "It was under Knight that Executive Editor Basil (Stuffy) Walters reshaped the *News*, eliminating its gray image and giving it a spicier 'bobby-sox' look. But even in bobby-sox, the *News* was still wearing football shoes to tromp on people who were stealing or oppressing the public." In the March 4, 1978, issue of *Editor and Publisher*, a former Chicago newsman named Budd Gore wrote, in "A Brief History of the *Daily News*," that Walters, "to the horror of the old timers, 'jazzed up' the paper, made it typographically exciting, gained new readers steadily."

What Walters actually did was simple: he made the *Daily News* more readable. He went from an all upper case Gothic typeface to headlines with caps and lower case. As in Minneapolis, he pumped in more white space, in part by fluctuating type styles in the same story. Asterisks were used to separate paragraphs in key parts of a story. (Once, when someone in Minneapolis who had lost track of Walters asked about him, the other person replied, "He's growing asterisks on a farm in Chicago.")

After Walters retired and became the first appointment to a new journalism chair at Syracuse University in 1972, he described the typographical changes in his second seminar before students and faculty members:

> The type and makeup we used were adaptations of those developed at Des Moines and Minneapolis after the Gallup survey and further refined during the planning Knight and I did at the *Detroit Free Press* during the summer preceding the purchase of the *News*. We had even printed a mockup, under the pretense we were planning it for the *Free Press*, and so we had a pattern ready for use by staff members. The resulting product won the *Daily News* the Inland Daily Press award year after year.

The initial changes in the *Daily News* weren't all cosmetic. Walters knew that content and clarity would have to change quickly, too.

Budd Gore, in his sparse *Editor and Publisher* history of the *Daily*

News, wrote, "The quality of writing may have suffered, but business improved [after Knight and Walters assumed command]."

Indeed, from an intellectual standpoint, the writing quality may have suffered. But from a newspaper standpoint, where the average reading level was far below that of a high school graduate, the writing improved. Walters pushed the principles Gunning outlined in his book, *The Techniques of Clear Writing*. Editors push the same principles today: write to express, not impress; tie in with your readers' experience; use terms your readers can picture; use action verbs; avoid unnecessary words; prefer the familiar word; keep sentences short; prefer the simple to the complex.

Knight and Walters posted a note on the bulletin board: "Short leads and short sentences. No lead is to be more than three typewritten lines, two if possible." Knight set an example in his weekly "Editor's Notebook." He used punchy, snappy short sentences. (His column won the Pulitzer Prize for editorial writing in 1968.)

Foreign service correspondents disagreed with Walters's and Knight's writing ideas. After Walters sent a memo on clear writing, one correspondent answered that he was writing for the University of Chicago and Northwestern professors. Goaded by this remark, Walters went to a University of Chicago faculty meeting with a batch of foreign service copy. He found that even the professors did not readily understand some of the pretentious prose.

Walters and Knight went beyond that test to demonstrate that their ideas were correct. Studies at the time showed that the average adult's reading speed was comparatively slow. They sent Howard Vincent O'Brien, a *Daily News* columnist, to the University of Chicago to take a reading test. O'Brien was a Yale graduate and one of the best read men on the *Daily News* staff. But the test given by the Adult Reading Clinic under the auspices of the School of Education, showed that O'Brien had ninth-grade reading ability.

"I had long suspected that I was a slow reader, but I was hardly prepared for what the movie of my eye movements revealed," O'Brien told *Editor and Publisher* in April 1946. "Instead of proceeding from one group of words to another, as normal eyes should, mine hesitate, jump from word to word ... and then jumped back to start the process over again. I am long on 'fixations,' short on number of words fixed ... ."

O'Brien scored seventy percent on central thought, that is, understanding about three-fourths of what he read. But he slipped to fifty percent when tested on details. He scored eighty percent on interpretation, but dropped when tested on integration of ideas to only forty-two percent.

Walters said such research studies "are bringing a new thought into editorial circles generally. The thought is that there is not necessarily a relationship between intelligence and ability to read. Also, there are indications that the use of type, or rather the misuse of type, is involved in the failure to attract and hold readers."

The *Editor and Publisher* article gave an example of how more "eye appeal" was being achieved with shorter leads. The lead of a story written in August 1945 on the War Manpower Commission appeared this way:

> A crew of 20 specially trained men to assist in interregional recruiting of 96,000 workers needed in the next two months for the lagging munitions programs will be dispatched from Washington to areas including Illinois, the War Manpower Commission (WMC) revealed today.

Editor and Publisher reported that this is the way the *Daily News* jumps into a WMC story today:

> Some 20,000 workers were needed December 1 for critical duty in Chicago. Today the requirement has been reduced to 16,200.

Managing Editor Norlander told the magazine, "We are trying to publish a paper that is interesting, authoritative, fair and honest. We recognize that newspapers are not always written at a readability level for the average person, so we are trying to make the *Daily News* easier to understand."

The local staff supported Knight and Walters for the most part, especially after editors were told that the foreign staff must compete for space with all other news available, whether it be from the wire services, the Washington bureau, or locally produced. With the exception of a powerful few who were foreign service-oriented, the local editors were delighted. Thus local staffers, whose copy was no longer being written for the wastepaper basket, rallied behind the new program. The once-powerful few left.

It was a foreign story, however, that produced Walters's first big splash in Chicago.

Despite his tremendous patriotism, Walters generally refused to cooperate when the Central Intelligence Agency asked him to be more permissive in allowing the agency to use *Daily News* correspondents. He felt strongly about compromising the paper's integrity by getting involved with government intelligence activities. But one exception led to a famous exclusive on the Ciano Diaries.

Raleigh Warner, a *Daily News* company director, came to Knight's Office shortly after Knight's purchase and said the Office of Strategic Services (OSS) was trying to get the diaries of Count Ciano, Italian Prime Minister Benito Mussolini's son-in-law. Ciano had been executed by the Fascists after going over to the Allied side. Absolute secrecy must be preserved, Warner cautioned.

Allied and German intelligence officials were searching madly for the diaries, which contained strategic details of the plans Germany and Italy had developed to defeat the Allies. Only the Count's widow, Edda, knew the diaries were buried in a garden in northern Italy. The count had revealed that shortly before his execution in January 1944. He also told her about John Whittaker, who represented the *Daily News* in Rome. Whittaker, before being killed as a soldier in the war, had told Ciano that if he decided to publish the diaries he should offer them to the *Daily News*.

After her husband's death, Edda found the diaries. When she crossed the Swiss border for asylum in a Swiss monastery, she carried the diaries strapped to her body under her clothing, which made her look pregnant.

Edda would talk only to representatives of the *Daily News*, the OSS learned. Knight assigned Walters to the project. Without legal advice, Walters drew up an offer for world publishing rights and advanced $10,000 to be delivered by the OSS in Geneva to Paul Ghali, a *Daily News* correspondent, for payment to Edda. A substantial additional payment was to be made later.

The OSS was to handle the transmission of the diaries to the United States and deliver either the diaries or copies and translation to Walters, with the understanding that the OSS participation remain secret for several years.

Walters was advised to visit Washington. He asked if he could include foreign editor Hal O'Flaherty in the secret. He could. In Washington, the two men were led into a windowless room and given a large volume of typewritten sheets. There was no desk in the room. The two men had to hold the book between them and read simultaneously, frequently changing sides to relieve tired arms.

It was all revealed before their eyes — the eyewitness story of the Hitler-Mussolini alliance by a man who was present at their meetings and who frequently was an envoy.

Walters and O'Flaherty were told they could pick up a translation and copy of the microfilm in a week. A week later they went back to Washington and found resistance at the OSS reception desk. There was no explanation. Walters worried. The European war was drawing to a close; the diaries' value would be greatly diminished if there should be a long delay in securing them. He and O'Flaherty returned to Chicago.

Ten days passed. The *Daily News*'s business office asked Walters to account for the $10,000. Knight fronted for his editor. On the eleventh day after Walters's and O'Flaherty's second trip to Washington, Walters found two small tin cans containing microfilm on his desk. He had returned to it after being away for only a few minutes to visit the newsroom. He never learned how the microfilm got there.

Walters called Northwestern University and arranged for

translators. He contacted his old pals at the Register and Tribune Syndicate in Des Moines. They undertook the sale to other newspapers for publication to start the next week.

The *Daily News* simply announced that the diaries had been obtained by Ghali from Edda Ciano. Walters and O'Flaherty vouched for their authenticity. The worldwide sale exhausted all potentials within the week. Fascinating details of Hitler's and Mussolini's war and political strategies were soon pouring across the globe.

Walters was not through, however. There was the additional payment to Edda — and it proved difficult to complete. Restrictions on the transfer of money abroad were in effect. Technically, Edda was an alien enemy. If the *Daily News* made too much fuss, the money would be seized. But the paper was determined to live up to the agreement John Whittaker had made with her years before. An agent finally reached her with the additional cash.

That kind of scoop was needed. The *Times* had topped the *Daily News* — for one month, October 1944, the month Knight took over.

The slide was quickly halted. Within one year, the *Daily News* fought its way to second place, trailing only McCormick's *Tribune*, which had built a substantial lead over the entire field. In a year, starting September 30, 1944, the *Daily News* grew from a circulation of 421,418 to 461,602. This was a tremendously successful twelve months under Knight. In a front-page signed editorial, "After One Year," Knight noted that for September 1945, the daily net average was 479,840, an increase of 44,892 over September 1944.

Knight took that opportunity to reiterate the aims he had announced when he assumed control: (1) to keep the *Daily News* politically independent; (2) to insist that the newspaper's first responsibility is to the general public — uncontrolled by any group, faction, or special interest; (3) to fight for those principles the *Daily News* believes to be right and resist any encroachment upon the liberties and inalienable rights of people; and (4) to serve as an impartial portrayer of the news, a fearless interpreter of the moving events of our times, and a faithful, sincere, and honest servant of the people.

Meanwhile, Hearst watched his *Herald-American* fall from second place. The *Daily News* had chewed away a lead of about 60,000. Impressed, Hearst approached Walters and offered him a job in his vast publishing empire. Starting yearly salary: $150,000. Walters said no, telling the press czar, as tactfully as he could, that he didn't want to be part of Hearst's sensationalism.

"Besides," Walters recalled in retirement, "I was having too much fun with the *Daily News*. Jack Knight was one of the swellest guys you could work for."

Knight's foreign correspondents didn't think Walters was swell. He was reshaping the service Victor Lawson had put together after Melville Stone first hatched the idea because of the lack of accurate reports on the Spanish-American War.

For years, the *Daily News*'s service was not only the first, but the finest. By the time Walters and Knight arrived, however, it had slipped. Some bright lights were still around, but, to a large degree, the service was riding on its reputation. Walters and Knight saw beyond the reputation. As Nixon Smiley wrote in his book on the history of the *Miami Herald (Knights of the Fourth Estate)*, Knight looked upon the *News*' (foreign) coverage as merely voluminous and dull. He wanted a newspaper that would be read. This meant brighter, succinct writing and the discouragement of long, ponderous articles. In Walters he had selected an editor who could make changes, and gradually they were made.

Foreign correspondents weren't the only people who complained about the changes. Carl Sandburg was so angered he refused to enter the *News* building. While he and Walters remained friends, they would often argue over the changes.

Some readers squawked, too. Smiley wrote in his book, "When a foreign policy dilettante demanded to know why Knight no longer attempted to produce the kind of paper that Frank Knox had published, Knight snapped: 'If this paper had continued to be edited as it was, there wouldn't be any *Daily News*.'"

Some observers wondered whether Walters actually wanted to dismantle the foreign service or reshape it. They noted that Walters was dedicated to rebuilding local coverage. But Walters proved that killing the foreign service had never entered his mind. He merely wanted to apply the successful ideas of George Gallup and Robert Gunning to the foreign dispatches, enabling readers to relate to stories whether they came from Boston or Bombay.

Walters even got involved in the sales efforts, resulting in new clients. By 1957, twelve years after concentrated effort, *Newsweek* wrote in a story about Walters:

> The once-ill CDN service ... is getting healthy. Currently it has 57 subscribers, more than ever before. Moreover, there are those who contend that the *New York Times*' recent effort to brighten its overseas copy was a result of grudging appreciation for the Knight-Walters system. Characteristically, Walters is not satisfied. "I'd like to make it a hundred clients before I retire in five years," he says, and unstuffy Stuffy may do it. "Edit everything that needs it," he once instructed a *Daily News* department head. "And that goes for everybody's copy — even John S. Knight's."

Walters fell short of getting 100 clients, but made significant progress. When Knight bought the *Daily News*, there were thirty-eight clients. When Walters retired in 1962, the foreign service had sixty-two clients and, at times, the figure approached seventy.

The growth was accomplished by not only improving the service's quality, but also with strong promotion. The *Daily News* published a large promotional advertisement November 29, 1955, that also appeared later on the cover of *Editor and Publisher*. Walters was the focus. Outlined by a map of different foreign countries patched together, Walters — cigar in mouth, glasses firmly in place, phone to left ear, usual smile of delight on his face — sat in his overstuffed office chair. That same photo appeared much smaller in the middle of the map, with lines running from the smaller photo to the larger photo. That was the top half of the ad.

A headline separating the photo from the text below said, "Dig for the Significant." The copy began:

> "He is as modern as TV and contemporary architecture.... He can smell propaganda right through 3,000 miles of ocean cable." In this way, recently, Publisher John S. Knight described the executive editor of the *Chicago Daily News* and the director of its famed Foreign Service ... Basil L. (Stuffy) Walters.

Later in the copy, a paragraph proclaimed:

> Stuffy does not crush his correspondents with fatuous rules. "Dig for the significant ... tell it interestingly" is his key instruction. And all on his staff are aware that their aim is not so much to tell WHAT happened — since the news agencies do this — but to tell HOW and WHY it happened and what it MEANS.

The ad proclaimed that the foreign service had "the largest assignment desk in the world...."

The *Daily News* Foreign Service Walters directs — America's oldest — is bought and published by more than 50 big-newspaper editors across the nation ... all linked to Stuffy by 6,593 miles of leased wire. It was strictly a Walters idea to accept "hunches" for timely stories from these distinguished editors along his wire. Result: His assignment desk has become literally the largest in existence — a clearing point for story suggestions sparked by America's top editors from coast to coast.

Walters always looked for a "spectacular attention getter" for the service — even as late as 1959, after Marshall Field, Jr. bought the *Daily News* from Knight. Walters, who had agreed to remain with Field, wrote him a memo on April 7, giving him details on a foreign service "spectacular" so the new publisher "will have the background of the methods we have employed in building a solid list of wire clients."

Walters told Field the service planned to send reporter John Smith to Australia with a farmer named Yankus to show how agricultural controls there compare with those in the United States. Walters wrote in his memo:

> We haven't had a man in Australia for some time. We try to have people in every important part of the world two or three times a year and time the visits to fit in the coverage with some event which creates public interest in the area. This type of thing seems to have worked out as quite a suitable program for a supplemental foreign service. We have felt for some time that we need at this stage some sort of rather spectacular attention getter to the foreign service. This seems to be the best bet now available.

The memo's last four paragraphs illustrate Walters's selling techniques and his understanding of editors and egos. He wrote to Field:

> I used the prospective Yankus trip as an excuse to discuss our foreign service with Gene Pulliam last night. It is not available to his Indianapolis papers because his competition has it, but it is available in Arizona (where Pulliam owned papers).
> Gene said his foreign editor, Michael Padev, had told him frequently that the CDN service is tops of all the supplemental services. The problems of selling a top man is the danger of offending the managing editor. If a managing editor feels there has been an end-run to the boss, the sale usually doesn't last beyond the original contract period. I'll call my friend, Harry Montgomery, assistant to the publisher at Phoenix, at the right time, and offer him the Yankus trip stories for free and then later I'm sure we will have an excellent chance of getting

the wire into Phoenix.

The *Daily News* sought new foreign service clients by periodically sending promotional material to editors. A four-page letter, single-spaced and making ample use of Walters's beloved asterisks, was sent January 5, 1956, under Walters's signature. The letter reads like an "advance" story newspapers write before a major event or meeting. The letter lays out the world scene as 1956 opens, working in the views of foreign service correspondents, such as the famed Keyes Beech. Midway through the letter, Walters writes, "We are watching the Middle East particularly this year. Russia is fishing in troubled waters there. Oil is of course the great prize, but the Asiatic countries are showing signs of interest in industrialization and modernization."

The fear that some had over the foreign service's future eventually faded. Walters wanted more local news, but he had never ignored the international scene and wasn't about to in Chicago. In fact, the truly major stories in Walters's first few years came from overseas. On May 8, 1945, eight months after arriving in Chicago, Walters watched his staff put together a front page reporting the Nazi surrender and the seizing of top German leaders Hermann Goering and Heinrich Himmler. A short dispatch from Paris, by the foreign service's Helen Kirkpatrick, led off the page, reporting how Admiral Doenitz seized control of the German government before it finally fell.

On August 7, 1945, the *Daily News* devoted most of its front page to the atomic bomb being dropped on Hiroshima. And a week later, the *News* dragged out three-inch headline type for "War Ends."

Again, most of the front page was related to Japan's surrender, including a small United Press story out of San Francisco. It ran at the bottom of the page. The headline: "V-J Fun Has Everything — Even 2 Nude Beauties." Two nude women had stepped from a taxi near the civic center servicemen's dormitory and plunged into the center's lily pond. The servicemen applauded as the women briefly cavorted. Then they emerged, gratefully accepted towels, re-entered the taxi and were seen no more. It was the kind of story Walters loved, the kind that had "Page One" written all over it.

A year later, August 6, 1946, a local story with tremendous impact broke. William Heirens, a seventeen-year-old University of Chicago student, confessed before State's Attorney William J. Tuohy that he had murdered six-year-old Suzanne Degnan, ex-Wave Frances Brown, and Mrs. Josephine Ross, a widow.

Reporter Alfred Prowitt's opinion was allowed to creep into the main news story. He wrote:

> Calmly, without hesitation, he gave full details of his shocking crimes before a circle of police officials in Tuohy's office.
>
> But at times his glance fell to the floor as if he were ashamed of the brutal acts he had committed.

Prowitt quoted Heirens as saying he "strangled her (Suzanne) as she lay in her bed." Then, using short, staccato paragraphs — the Walters style — Prowitt described, with some sensationalism, how Heirens killed the young girl. Here's a touch of his story:

> "How long did you keep your hands on her neck, would you say?"
> "About two minutes."
> "You squeezed as hard as you could?"
> "Until everything went limp."

Bobby Knight is complex and misunderstood

Michigan City *News-Dispatch*, Dec. 10, 1982

When I learned that a prominent Michigan City optometrist was a close friend of controversial Indiana University basketball coach Bobby Knight, I decided to have a chat with him. It turned into a long interview, resulting in this column.

It's summer 1972, and Bobby Knight is sitting alone in a corner — a nobody.

Knight, who has just completed his first basketball season at Indiana University with a solid 17-8 record, is relaxing at a gathering of IU athletic department people and supporters.

Suddenly, out of the smoke and the noise and the back patting, a Michigan City eye doctor approaches the solitary Knight.

"Coach," the doctor says with a wide grin, "you think you'll ever amount to anything?"

Bobby Knight, the *enfant terrible*, silently tosses back a wide grin of his own.

An exceptionally close friendship is launched.

Optometrist Carl Golightly sits in the examining room of his office on Washington Street and quickly makes one thing clear: Those who feel that Bobby Knight is a tyrant are off base.

Some people feel that Knight is untamed. They cite ugly behavior on and off the basketball court. They contend that while two NCAA championships and an NIT crown prove Knight is an all-time winner as a coach, his behavior makes him a loser as a human being.

Golightly admits that at times when he reads something negative about Knight he winces. He admits, too, that his first response is to be protective toward the coach.

"But most importantly," the doctor adds, "I put the criticism into perspective, knowing Knight and knowing the likelihood of the accuracy.

Sometimes I say, 'Yeah, that's Bob.' Sometimes I say, 'Hey, the guy (being critical) is off base.' I can see how people misunderstand Bobby, because he is such a complex individual."

He's more than that. He's also "intense, volatile, very bright and a man with a strong sense of purpose ... and he's sensitive almost to a fault," Golightly says.

A lifelong sports nut who received his bachelor's and optometry degrees from IU in the early '60s, Golightly has associated with athletes and coaches his entire life. He has helped Hoosier coaches with recruiting for years.

Knight is not only the smartest coach he has ever observed, he's also the straightest recruiter, the doctor says.,

Shortly after that party 10 years ago, Golightly said, he discovered in a telephone call that Knight was "death on the rules even when he was a nobody."

At the party, Golightly told Knight he thought Elston's towering center, Al Fleming, was outstanding. Knight agreed.

"So when it got late in the recruiting season and I didn't hear from Knight, I called him, having naively thought Bobby would call me," Golightly related with a chuckle. "Bobby said, 'Thank you very much, doctor. We don't ask alumni to do any of our recruiting.' And he hung up.

"Needless to say, I was miffed. So I went back to seeing my patients. Ten minutes later, he called back and said, 'Doctor, I'm sorry if I was rude, but we really do not allow our alumni to get involved in our recruiting. However, I will be in Michigan City this week and I'd like to explain our program and get any information from you.'"

Fleming chose Arizona, where he had a fine collegiate career. Knight used the opening to select Tom Abernethy, who played on the Hoosiers' 1976 NCAA championship team and continues as a pro today.

"What you see and what you get with Bobby Knight is very consistent," Golightly says. "But unless you are a Bobby Knight-watcher, it's confusing.

"I think he has very good control of himself' and has come to grips with some of his personality and used it to develop his own persona."

What about the swearing and yelling at his players? What about that incident a few seasons back, when he gained nationwide notoriety by grabbing Jim Wisman's jersey as the player came off the floor during a time out? What about the international incident Knight helped cause as coach of the U.S. team in the 1979 Pan American games, when he was found guilty in absentia after a brouhaha with a Puerto Rican policeman?

"His tirades at the officials and the press and his volatile nature are calculated," Golightly responds.

"If you watch Indiana players come off the floor, he'll yell at them, but as they huddle, he's all business. You'll never see him get a technical in a crucial situation. I would guess that half the technicals he gets are calculated or shouldn't have been called by the referee.

"As for the Puerto Rican thing, it was a calculated political stunt by a policeman who was a part-time law student. The guy deliberately precipitated the event to discredit Knight and the United States basketball program. People present said Knight did not slug the policeman and the policeman deliberately overreacted to draw attention. It was all a bum rap."

Knight sees himself as a teacher, and Golightly says that's "no phoney baloney." He marvels at Knight's attention to detail, citing the recruiting program as an example.

Knight gathers a list of about 50 top prospects, compared to most coaches' lists of 100 to 150. He sends each prospect — almost everyone comes from the Indiana/Illinois/Ohio recruiting area — a questionnaire to see if he is interested in IU. Knight develops a priority list from those who respond.

"He will only recruit the kids who have A, character; B, scholarship and C, athletic ability," Golightly says. "He will determine what his team's needs are by type of player and recruit to his needs. And he will concentrate on a small and select number of kids."

Knight does not believe in long romances. If he does not get a prospect quickly, he will move on to his other choices.

"Many coaches will run all over the USA telling all the kids they're after they're wonderful, and many times those coaches will get caught in a trap because players they really want don't commit soon enough," Golightly said. "So, they get stuck with some players not as high on their priority list.

"Or, a kid thinks a school is dead serious and he stops checking other schools. The school he thought he was going to sign with winds up not taking him and the kid is left hanging.

"Recruiting is like a selection of dances—getting the right partner. You don't over-recruit kids unless you really intend to take them. Knight is always up front with his intentions."

Knight's penchant for details extends to who is allowed to sit behind the IU bench. If you have tickets for that select locale, be prepared for a student manager to approach you before the game and "make sure you're legit."

The doctor chuckles. "And Bobby likes to warn who is sitting there to watch out for flying chairs."

That kind of behavior—checking the seat occupants—is indicative of a cold, insecure man, Knight's critics might say.

"I know there's a feeling that Bobby is cold and anti-women," Golightly says, "but he's really warm and not anti-women. He has a very good marriage. His wife (Nancy) and his family are very involved with the basketball program. Nancy is an integral part of Bobby's basketball camp in the summer.

"She understands her role in keeping the family together during the hectic basketball season. I've been fortunate enough to stay in their home overnight and to see that they are warm, solid people."

Knight showed great kindness to Landon Turner, the 6-10 forward who played brilliantly as a junior and appeared headed for professional stardom only to have his career snapped in an automobile accident the summer before his senior year.

Some Knight-haters might feel Turner's case is the exception, not the rule, with Knight. When Golightly is asked about this possibility, he ticks off acts of kindness.

Last Aug. 14, he recalled, he was in Knight's office when the IU mentor called Willis Reed, the former New York Knicks great, who was starting his first year of coaching at Creighton University in Omaha.

"Bobby told him to get his practice schedule firmed up and fly to Weir Cook (Indianapolis International Airport), and that he would pick him up," Golightly recalled.

"He told Reed, 'You'll spend the night with me and I'll set aside a couple of days for us to sit down so I can explain our total concept in building a basketball program.'

"If you hang around Knight's office long enough, you will see a parade of high school and college coaches coming and going."

Knight reportedly is extremely demanding at practice sessions, frequently blistering his players with harsh language not fit for a family newspaper.

Golightly confirms that Knight is a no-nonsense disciplinarian, but notes that after his players leave IU, they return to Bloomington and help in a variety of ways. They attend to help or recognize others, such as Turner, or they sit on the bench during a crucial game, or they play a role that assists the basketball program.

"You talk about kindness...," Golightly says. "Knight will negotiate a player's contract if the player wants him to. The players always have access to him. He has a lawyer that sets up the contract for the player and charges only on an hourly rate, so the standard 10 percent agent fees don't apply to his players' future contracts."

Shortly after the 1976 championship year, when Scott May was the top player in the country, Knight called Golightly and asked if he was free for lunch. Golightly was. Knight replied, "I'm on the Toll Road heading for Chicago; I'll stop by your office."

Knight arrived and went to Golighty's phone. He called Arthur Wirtz, whose family owns the Chicago Bulls, and said he was prepared to make a final offer on May's behalf. Either the Bulls accept it, or Knight would send May to Italy or put him on his staff for a year until the next pro draft. "I'm leaving Michigan City and either going west (to Chicago) or south (to Bloomington)," he told Wirtz.

Knight went to Chicago. The Bulls signed May to a hefty six-figure pact.

Knight also looks after his former assistant coaches. Once IU has its quota of recruits, Knight and his staff help ex-associates.

As I chatted with Golightly in his examining room one recent morning, the phone rang. It was former top assistant Bob Donewald, now at Illinois State, calling to get background on a Michigan City prospect.

"When someone like Donewald asks me about a kid, I call high school coaches who played against the kid," Golightly quickly points out. "I gather the reports and send them along to the coach. I'm not the basketball expert."

Golightly pauses, then turns to another part of Knight's personality — the side that loves to pull practical jokes on people and vice versa.

"One day I get a call from Bobby, and he says, 'Carl, I need a favor,' and I fell for it," Golightly smiled broadly. "I replied, 'Bob, what do you want?' And he said, 'I need someone to go to Puerto Rico for me.' It was right after the incident down there."

It's obvious that Golightly would do about anything for Knight — even when not asked. When the doctor learned that "60 Minutes" was preparing a segment on Knight, he wrote a fan letter to the producers,

Told about it, Knight fussed, "I don't give a damn what they say about me."

Golightly replied: "Bob, the letter was intended to get publicity for *me*."

Golightly, of course, was tweaking Knight. The doctor, in fact, had written to 60 Minutes in all sincerity on Knight's behalf, without the coach's knowledge.

"60 Minutes" chose not to use Golighty's brief note. If the program had, Bobby Knight — the nobody who became a somebody — would have been summed up succinctly in these Golightly words:

"Being loved is not one of his needs, being easily understood is not one of his blessings, but being respected is mandatory."

Memories of pancakes, pot pies, simple joys

News-Dispatch, Michigan City, May 6, 1983

A Mother's Day column about my Yiddish mamala.

When the evening shadows fall
And the lovely day is through
And with longing I recall
The years I spent with you...
Mama ...

I hear Connie Francis sing those lyrics and think about Saturday morning pancakes and Dr Pepper after school and the "shopping game" and buying clothes in the fall and chicken pot pie and a few bills being stuffed in my pocket and being held in her chunky, 4-foot-9 body and being *loved*.

Sunday will mark the sixth year she has not been with us for her day — and frankly, I won't be thinking more about her Sunday than I do the other 364 days, because, it seems, I think of her more and more as I grow older.

I think, sometimes, of the days when I came home from school in the second grade and would occasionally get a treat: a bottle of Dr Pepper. It was my favorite, and she knew it — and we both knew that a bottle of soda pop was a luxury for a family that didn't have a lot of loose change to spare those days. But she got such a simple joy out of my simple joy.

I think, sometimes, about when I was 9 years old and she would take me to the big department stores, where we always had lunch — and without fail, she ordered chicken pot pie, getting such a simple joy from turning over the steaming casserole dish and emptying the crust-covered contents on her plate.

I think, sometimes, about a day she would set aside shortly before school started in the fall so she could take me out for clothes — and the simple joy she got out of selecting plaid shirts and later Levis, and always brown Oxfords.

I think, sometimes, of my teen years, when things were better for us, and she quietly put a few dollar bills in my pants pocket before I went out on a Friday night and I could hear her simple joy when she said, "Have fun, Ramey."

I think, sometimes, of Saturday morning breakfast, which was always pancakes, stack after stack, until I was about to burst — and the simple joy she got from plopping those tasty "panners" onto my plate from the big black skillet.

I think, sometimes, of how she would ask me to drive her to the cleaners — just the cleaners — but I would wind up driving her to the cleaners, two supermarkets, the drug store and a delicatessen, complaining all the way — and whereas I once felt guilty about my complaining, now I get a simple joy when I think about the "shopping game," because it reminds me how she could manipulate me so easily ... and I am glad she could.

And the love. I think all the time about the love. It came at me no matter my behavior, continuously coated me and carved positive things into my soul — and all so simply.

Such simple things, such simple joys, that it didn't occur to me until just a few days ago that I had shortchanged her.

For years, when occasionally asked if there had been any people who had a strong influence on my life, I replied: "Yes, three," and I would talk about three men, one of whom was my father.

I should have been saying, "Yes, four," all along. But she was so easy to overlook, so easy because she was such a simple, basic, loving human being, filled with devotion and protectiveness, dedicated to making me and my brother and my two sisters the best human beings she possibly could. She was so ordinary, she was extraordinary, but it did not show, until just the other day, when I said, "Yes, three," and it hit me, suddenly, and for a moment I felt dumb, but then, quickly, felt good, because I had discovered something important.

Come Sunday, for those of you who think, sometimes, like I think about that unique human being who is a cornerstone of your life, don't forget that the ordinary is often extraordinary.

Safe in the glow of your love
Sent from the heavens above
Nothing can ever replace
The warmth of your tender embrace
Oh, Mama, until the day
That we're together once more
I'll live in these memories
Until the day that we're
Together once more

A little less arrogance, a little more credibility

Michigan City *News-Dispatch*, July 8, 1983

Straight talk in a column on the relationship between newspapers and readers.

We come into this business with thin skin. We are a breed that doesn't take criticism easily. We hunch our backs, like a cat sensing danger, when someone questions our performance. We are insecure because our bylines and/or our titles reveal to the world who goofed on what. We wrap ourselves inside the First Amendment.

David Shaw, the *Los Angeles Times'* respected media critic, thinks that the "gravest ethical problem confronting the press today is our own arrogance—our hypocritical resentment of questions and criticism, our insularity...our refusal to be held accountable for our shortcomings, large or small."

Well, you say, newspaper people are no different from anyone else. After all, criticism is a fact of life in all walks of life, and no one likes to be criticized.

Agreed. But those of us who purvey information need to learn how to accept criticism more gracefully if we are to improve our performance. We need to dismantle our walls of defensiveness.

Common sense tells us to shed the thin skin and grow thick skin. If we don't, we face a raft of personal and professional problems — and, most important, we don't grow.

Some of us — a minority — have been trying to do this for years. It is not always easy. And we are not perfect. But when someone lodges a legitimate complaint honestly and sincerely, we do not feel the discomfort we once did. We make a correction if need be and try harder the next time. If we've made an error of omission, we try to rectify it as best we can.

Sometimes, though, the intemperance we are rightly accused of is used on us. Two months ago, for example, I received a letter which said we made a mistake. We had. A correction was printed the next day.

The letter-writer, however, also listed alleged past sins and wrote: "...your articles sometimes have the quality of writing that one might expect of 2nd graders."

That assertion is hyperbolic, and I said so in responding to the letter writer.

It is hard to respond calmly at times like that. The urge to return insult for insult is great. As we grow older, though, we mellow, and that helps keep us from sinking to our attacker's level.

The mellowing process, however, is not enough. Journalists need to achieve a greater degree of self-honesty and a better understanding of people's emotions and frailties.

Now, having come clean with all that, let me say a few things about the public that journalists need to understand better. That public, in turn, needs to understand us better.

Those we serve should begin with the realization that we are human beings who make mistakes like all human beings. And because all human beings make mistakes, some errors that appear in the *News-Dispatch* are caused because erroneous information was given to us.

Because none of us is perfect human beings, we ought to accept mistakes to a certain degree. Obviously, if someone keeps making mistakes, corrective action must be taken, perhaps to the point of dismissal.

Mistakes aside, we are accused of some things that don't take place — or, if they do, very rarely and are committed by people who better not get caught if they want to keep their jobs.

For example, we don't print a story or leave out a story or blow up story or play down a story because someone out there knows someone in here. The old saying, "It's not what you know, it's who you know," doesn't apply at this newspaper.

Frankly, I don't have a lot of close friends outside the newspaper business. And the ones I do have won't ask me for a favor if they know I will have to compromise my principles. That's why they are close friends.

Well, you say, what about others in the news department? Can't they do favors for someone without you knowing? Of course. But they don't. At least I haven't seen any strong evidence. I don't monitor possible favoritism closely because I believe we have people whose principles of honest and responsible journalism match mine.

We are also accused of doing certain things because an advertiser is involved. We don't. Yes, it gets uncomfortable on some rare occasions. But mature, intelligent, ethical people understand some basic truths, such as:

On the one hand, we need advertisers, because their support — their dollars — determine how good a product we can deliver. The more advertising we sell, the more pages we have for news. On the other hand, our advertisers need us. We help them sell their goods and services.

We both need credibility; it's absolutely vital. If we are dictated to by advertisers, we are not credible, and if we are not credible, our advertisers, by association, are not credible; their goods and services are called into question.

In the final analysis, as a newspaper we must be believed by our public (which includes our advertisers). When we are believed, our advertisers are believed — and the public's trust in us as a medium that serves this community leads to a trust of our advertisers' goods and services.

Thus, while we can never compromise ourselves to an advertiser, we must respect our advertisers, just as we must respect our readers, just as we must respect ourselves.

Which gets me to the accusation that we cover up things.

We don't. Sometimes we miss stories or sometimes we're a day or two or even a week behind because we don't have essential information. Our staff does a solid job of covering the community; I wouldn't hesitate to compare our local report with any newspaper our size. But — again — we are human, and sometimes things get by us. But we do not cover up for anyone. Period.

So where does all this leave us? Simply here: We in the newspaper business must learn to accept honest, constructive, sincere criticism without hiding behind the First Amendment, rationalizing our errors and/or becoming arrogant and smug toward our accusers.

In turn, the public must understand that the *News-Dispatch*, like the vast majority of newspapers, does not serve special interests, does not cover up news, does not slant stories — but does strive for accuracy and fairness.

One more thing: As journalists, we must realize that there is a minority of nasties in the world who will complain no matter what, while the public must realize that there are some journalists who will mess things up no matter what.

As someone once said, nobody's perfect.

Don't underestimate Richard Nixon's savvy, skill

Nixon Newspapers, May 1984

A column written after the annual convention of the American Society of Newspaper Editors in Washington about someone I personally didn't admire.

Someone sent the column to Nixon. I received a note from someone on his staff, along with a copy of his latest book, *Real Peace*. It was signed simply, "Richard Nixon." An autopen was probably used.

The book was not a major tome; I skimmed through it. After a few years, I gave it and a few others to a local library.

In a particularly important election year, it seems obvious that Ronald Reagan would gladly accept an invitation to appear before the prestigious American Society of Newspaper Editors (ASNE).

At the same time, while it has been 10 years since Watergate soiled American history, it seems obvious that Richard Nixon would reject an invitation to appear before the same organization.

So when ASNE's program committee issued invitations, Ronald Reagan said no and Richard Nixon said yes.

That was the first surprise. The second was Nixon's winning appearance. A man who has had a hate affair with the media all of his political life, he captured his audience with a foreign affairs speech dipped in statesmanship.

As in the past, ASNE invited the four presidential candidates to appear during its four-day gathering. Invitations were also extended to the three former chiefs.

Mondale said yes, Hart said no, Jackson said no, then gave a last-minute yes, Jimmy Carter and Jerry Ford said no. Reagan said no, even during negotiations that took place while the convention was in progress. (He appeared at a convention of Realtors that took place at the same time.)

So there was Richard Nixon, the least likely of folks, arriving for dessert and then — looking tanned and healthy — standing before a microphone.

After being introduced by Vermont Royster, the legendary former editor of the *Wall Street Journal,* Nixon removed his watch and delivered extemporaneously an almost spellbinding speech.

Sure, he had either given the same speech, or parts of it, earlier, but his performance amazed even some of the severest Nixon-haters.

Many of us had never seen Nixon so relaxed. At times, it seemed like he was not speaking as a former president to the most powerful editors in the country, but as a visiting professor before a graduate-school class in foreign affairs.

Say what you want to about Richard Nixon and Watergate, but do not underestimate his overall intelligence, particularly his brilliance in foreign affairs. Nixon ought to be used by our government — Republican or Democrat — as some kind of foreign affairs consultant or representative.

But don't look for this happening — and that's too bad. He probably has the best background and understanding of anyone in the nation for dealing with foreign governments.

The Reagan administration could make great use of his skills in an area in which it has failed for the most part. But don't look for an invitation from the proud Reagan movers and shakers.

After Nixon left the head table, several editors and members of the working press converged on him. I watched from a distance, expecting him to keep moving toward the exit. But no, Nixon stood, smiled, chatted amicably with people who had been his tormentors for years.

I edged up to the tight knot around him and wound up serving as a five-foot, human resting stand for a boom microphone.

Would he accept a post as a roving ambassador? he was asked, "No," Nixon smiled, "you have to attend too many dinners."

It's possible — maybe even likely — that Nixon has worked for the administration behind the scenes in an advisory capacity, which is fine. But he would be even more effective out in the open as an ambassador or special representative.

After his speech, Nixon fielded questions. The session opened testily: The first questioner prefaced it by saying he was in the audience in 1973 when Nixon addressed another powerful newspaper group and declared, "I am not a crook," in referring to Watergate.

Then the question was posed: What was the most significant lesson he had learned from Watergate in relation to its impact on the presidency?

"I lived it at the time and lived it in my memories and recent broadcasts," he responded. "As far as I'm concerned, I've covered the subject as well as I can. I think 10 years of Watergate is enough. I'm concerned with the future, not the past."

That answer drew a smattering of applause.

At breakfast the next morning, a group of us debated whether he should have answered the question or taken the route he had. The "vote" was split. I supported Nixon's response, although I don't think we have received all of the important answers about Watergate.

But I don't believe the atmosphere was right for Watergate. Nixon had spoken on foreign affairs and the questioning should have followed along that line.

Nixon did, however, respond to a political question — the presidential race — and scored brilliantly.

Without hesitation, he said Mondale — assuming he gets the nomination as expected — would "bow toward women and not take one" because it wouldn't help him on the ticket. He already has "activist-type" women supporting him.

Continuing on the vice-presidential question, he predicted Mondale will take either Sen. Lloyd Bentsen of Texas or primary foe Gary Hart. Bentsen has to "be considered because of the importance of the Texas vote."

For Mondale to succeed, however, he will also have to concentrate on Ohio, Pennsylvania, Michigan, Illinois and New York — and here,

Bentsen would not help. But Hart would, because he reaches a broader constituency, according to some exit polls. Nixon added that if Kennedy and Johnson had the capability to get together, so do Mondale and Hart.

Then Nixon brought laughter when he said, "Now, since so many states are represented, let me give you a state-by-state analysis" for a Reagan-Mondale race.

Reagan will win all of the West, including Colorado (Hart's home state), because Reagan can wear cowboy boots, too. In the big states, Reagan will win California and Texas without question. Mondale would win, as of today, Minnesota (his home state), Maryland, Massachusetts and Michigan.

"The critical battleground, then," Nixon continued, "comes in other major states, and — hold it a minute — the South."

Nixon noted that Reagan carried Mississippi, Alabama, South Carolina, Kentucky, Tennessee, and Arkansas by 17,000 votes or less in 1980. If Jesse Jackson supports Mondale strongly and the black vote increases by 2 percent, it would mean those states would vote for Mondale rather than Reagan.

Nixon, rolled on without missing a beat. Mondale has a chance in Ohio and Pennsylvania because of double-digit unemployment. He sees the major battleground being Texas, Illinois and New York. Texas looks good for Reagan; but the black vote will be 90 percent for Mondale.

Nixon thinks the final vote will be very close, with Reagan winning, "because I think he is a better candidate."

Then, quickly, he added: "Oh, a word about debates. I know what debates can do for a candidate and what they can do to him. There will be debates and I would predict that, at this time, Mondale would probably win the debates, Reagan will win the audience."

Nixon said he wouldn't bet the ranch on a Reagan victory, but he would bet the main house, "and unless the economy goes down, I wouldn't even bet the outhouse on Mondale."

I wouldn't bet anything, at this point, on how a Reagan-Mondale race would turn out in November. But I would bet that Richard Nixon won some votes the other night for a higher ranking in presidential lists — Watergate or not.

Note: Nixon proved to be wrong on his election predictions. Mondale chose the first woman — Geraldine Ferraro — to be his running mate. And Reagan swamped Mondale, who won only his home state, Massachusetts, and the District of Columbia.

GenCorp: A time to talk

Wabash Plain Dealer, Sept. 20, 1984

Editorials can serve many functions — persuade, crusade, explain, criticize, praise. And sometimes, an editorial is needed to bring opposing forces together to discuss and work out solutions to differences that result in a win-win. Such was the case when I wrote this editorial that centered on the possibility of Wabash losing its largest — and longtime — employer, originally known as General Tire, which would have crippled the community.

The plant eventually closed, but not until several years after this editorial helped smooth the way for an agreement that kept the facility in operation with several hundred workers.

It has been almost 50 years since General Tire and Rubber Co. — now known as GenCorp — came to Wabash and grew as the city's largest employer.

Sadly, in a few weeks or months, General Tire — as it is still known by Wabash countians — may be no more, leaving hundreds unemployed and the ghost of a plant at the intersection of Stitt and Bond streets.

Unemployed workers and the ghost need not be. General Tire probably can never again employ the 1,500 it once did. But it can employ more than half that number, and, more importantly, can remain a vital part of Wabash's economy.

What's immediately needed is this: A meeting of company and union officials in which give and take, concrete assurances and mutual survival are discussed with straight talk.

This becomes more imperative each day as the current contract's expiration date, June 29, 1985, draws closer. It becomes more imperative as company officials write letters to union president Ernest Pack to reconsider a two-tier wage and benefits proposal the membership declined to discuss at its May 23 monthly meeting. It becomes more imperative as the union responds to the company letters saying it will not consider any new offers until the current contract expires.

What we have here is a communications problem. That can be a cliché, but it fits this deteriorating situation.

R. E. Garber, vice president of industrial relations, says in a letter dated Sept. 11 to Pack that he understands workers' fears: being transferred to jobs where their present wages and/or benefits would be reduced from the current level, a reduced insurance package, future company demands for lower benefits, no monetary benefits in return for an extension of the current contract.

Garber tries to allay those fears by writing in his letter: "I have no question in my mind that if you (Pack) and your committee were free to sit down with us at the negotiating table, we could in a short period of time resolve these two issues (job transfer and reduced insurance) in a mutually satisfactory manner."

However, several union members, who asked to speak anonymously, have told the *Plain Dealer* that they have heard similar company assurances in the past only to see such assurances not be kept.

So while the company keeps asking Pack to urge the membership to reconsider the two-tier proposal — it would provide for additional jobs for concessions — the membership keeps responding by saying it will do nothing until next June 29.

Unfortunately — and not just for the workers, but all of Wabash County — June 29 may be too late. By then, it's possible that the entire question will be moot, that General Tire will be gone, for all intents and purposes, if some kind of agreement can't be reached in the near future.

In his Sept. 11 letter to Pack, Garber begins: "I feel I have an obligation to you and to your union to make this *one last effort* (italics ours) to preserve the jobs of the presently working employees and to give an opportunity to our presently laid off employees to return to active employment."

That sounds to us that if GenCorp and the union can't reach some accord soon, the plant will become a mixing facility employing just 50 or so people.

If it sounds like we are buying an empty threat, so be it. But it's based partly on the fact that the same anonymous workers who say they've been lied to in the past admit that the chances are good that GenCorp will essentially shut down if some kind of new agreement is not reached.

As we said, though, such an economic tragedy need not happen.

We don't know who is right or who is wrong, who is partly right or who is partly wrong, who is talking mostly straight or who is talking mostly crooked.

All we know is that the two parties need to sit down and have some meaningful, honest communication before meaningful, honest communication becomes too late — before a staggering blow is dealt to Wabash County's future.

Tragedy sears our senses, too

Wabash Plain Dealer, June 25, 1985

Like all journalists who have been around for a while, I've been called cold, uncaring and a few other nasty things more than a few times. People are entitled to their opinion. But ...

Last week was horrible for Ronald Reagan, wonderful for the media, right?

While the President agonized over the continuing TWA hostage crisis, the murder of four Americans in El Salvador and the reminder in Frankfurt, Germany, how terrorists can seemingly strike anywhere with death-dealing savagery, editors and producers rubbed their hands with glee over all the powerful headlines and footage that would grab readers and viewers by the eyeballs. Right?

Wrong.

Yes, these are gut-wrenching days for the President, days when the news menu is filled with the stuff that sells newspapers and traps television viewers — bad news.

Professionally, we may initially react to such breaking stories by saying, "Oh, man, this is a great story," which, frankly, sounds callous. I'd guess that the same kind of professional reaction — and spurt of adrenalin — is triggered in doctors, lawyers and other professionals suddenly faced with something powerful and unusual.

But for those of us who are the messengers of bad news, the hostage drama, airport bombing, and cold-blooded killings tear at our guts, too.

Like all of our readers and viewers, we are not in the same position as the President, holding the fate of American lives in his hands and being the Commander in Chief of people who lost their lives in the blood of El Salvador.

But because it is our job to bring people the news does not mean that we are oblivious to the hostages' fear of the unknown and the pain growing out of crazed gunmen snuffing out lives of loved ones.

We are human, too.

A thick skin gets us through a news cycle with a high degree of detachment needed to provide honest, factual journalism. And yet, the skin is not so thick that, after the heat of battle, we do not feel remorse, anger and frustration — the same emotions that tear at the President and our readers — for what has just occurred.

We may recover more quickly, partly because another edition or newscast pushes us into that mode of action and neutrality, but the feelings leave a residue that roam around in our core.

We are human, too.

We have children and husbands and wives and sisters and brothers and aunts and uncles and grandparents. We have the same kind of familial love for them that the average person possesses.

We empathize with tragedy like anyone else. Because we are in the news business does not make us immune to the ugliness of life that constantly stalks our society.

The ugliness does not have to be in the form of criminal behavior. It can be a tornado or earthquake. It can be a typhoon, such as the one that recently struck Bangladesh, leaving thousands dead and thousands more homeless and starving.

It does not matter that we know few of the people who suffer tragedy, that for the most part they are simply names that come across the news wire.

They are people, flesh and blood and bones like us — and we cannot be oblivious to the sanctity of life.

We feel the pain in varying degrees. Familiarity, kinship and nationality cause us to feel less grieved, frankly, for the victims of starvation in Ethiopia than we do for the Americans held hostage. And to feel less for the washed away in Bangladesh than for the Americans blasted to death in El Salvador.

But we feel for all, to some degree.

Still, we go on with our jobs, trying to keep rapidly unfolding events in balance and perspective, trying to shunt our feelings aside until the newspaper is on the streets or the newscast is on the air.

But we do not — cannot — go untouched.

We are only human, too.

Learning the hard way

Wabash Plain Dealer, March 18, 1986

After a news story reported that some parents at an elementary school in Wabash were upset with how a 6th-grade teacher taught apartheid, I wrote an editorial defending the teacher, David Hahn. I did not know Hahn.

More than 20 years later — now retired — I needed a new place to walk indoors during the harsh winter months in Indiana. I went to Blair Ridge Upper Elementary School in Peru, where I had lived for 17 years at the time, to see if I could walk there after school. I was directed to the office of Principal David Hahn. The name did not ring a bell with me.

After I made my request, Hahn said he lived in Wabash and knew who I was. He granted me permission. I still did not make a connection.

Some three years later, as I was going through myriad pieces I have written to determine which to include in this book, I came across the editorial. David Hahn's name jumped out at me. The connection finally hit me.

I have included this editorial not because I now count David Hahn as a friend, but because of the message it sends.

Some O.J. Neighbours parents are upset over a classroom experiment involving apartheid in South Africa.

The experiment conducted by teacher David Hahn involved dividing students into two groups — privileged and unprivileged. The students were chosen in a random drawing.

The experiment proved to be so realistic — the discrimination so strong — some students came home crying and upset. In turn, some parents became upset, which is understandable. They want learning to be a pleasant experience for their children.

But Hahn should not be cast in a negative light. If he is, he will fall victim — ironically — to what apartheid is fundamentally all about: unfairness.

The students admit that the experiment taught them something about life, even if it was at the expense of some friendships. But those friendships will heal quickly — if they haven't already.

Some of the privileged students admitted to *Plain Dealer* reporter Joseph Slacian that they took advantage of the unprivileged students. That's important to note. By admitting their actions, the privileged students showed that the lesson on unfair, bigoted behavior took hold.

It showed that they are young people who possess open minds. And without open minds that judge matters fairly, impartially and unemotionally, the world cannot become a better place in which to live.

The strongest lesson in the overall exercise may have been the final one: Only the privileged students were allowed to vote on whether to continue the experiment, because only the ruling class can decide on whether apartheid should continue.

Perhaps the experiment, conducted Monday through Wednesday, lasted a day or two too long. Perhaps Hahn should have notified the parents before it began. Certainly, the upsetting of some students is unfortunate.

But in the final analysis, the students — both the privileged and unprivileged — learned a vital lesson in life, one that will make them better human beings in a world that needs all the better human beings it can get.

When a tiny child grabs our hearts

Wabash Plain Dealer, Oct. 21, 1987

Sometimes columns write themselves. This was one did, and it will always be one of my favorites.

For 58 hours, while the Persian Gulf became more dangerous by the minute, while the stock market fell by the hour, while the football players' strike fizzled by the day, an 18-month-old girl held the nation by its collective heart.

And why not?

Is there anything more precious than a child? A babe in arms? A tiny bundle of love given life by an act — in most cases — of love?

In a world that is far too violent and far too impoverished in far too many places, it remains for a child to remind us that humanity can win if humanity wants to.

Men tunnel their way through solid rock, ignoring the searing earth heat that builds the longer they plow deeper toward a child alone and frightened in a dark, tiny crevice.

A businessman with no collarbones, who measures just 17 inches from shoulder to shoulder, volunteers to wiggle down the rescue hole, which measures just 18 inches, to lift the child.

Drill bits that cost thousand of dollars are brought in, broken and forgotten as Mother Earth, ironically, proves overly stubborn, as if she is trying to teach an old lesson.

A man talks to the child, soothing her, comforting her — and agonizing with her when she pleads for her Mommy.

From Maine to all points west, people send in ideas on how to save the child, including one that suggests bringing in a trained monkey from Hollywood to go down the rescue shaft and fetch her.

Neighbors provide food, prayer and whatever else they have that will ease the burden of those directly caught up in the battle for life and death.

Doctors stay on the scene, providing medical expertise, ensuring that the rescuers do not make a move that could prove life-threatening.

As the drama mounts, the media corps grows, and peoples of the world tune in, sending messages of hope and comfort.

And a mother and father wait, mostly indoors, unable to sleep and eat, their minds a jumble of fear and anxiety and appreciation and hope and second-guessing.

The rescue is successful and the child begins to receive hospital care, prompting an outpouring of stuffed animals, other gifts and well wishes.

For one child.

And why not?

That one child represents all children, represents, in the final analysis, us as a people as we strive to make tomorrow better, hoping and wishing and, for some of us, working for ways to reduce — if not halt — the agonies that confront us from the Gulf to Angola to Northern Ireland to Warsaw to South Africa to America's slums.

If men will put their personal safety on the line, if people will bring in expensive equipment without asking about dollars, if experts will contribute their medical minds, if peoples of different colors and faiths and races can get caught up in the fear and hope of a child and her parents—then that one child becomes an inspiration to us if we regularly reflect on who we are, what we stand for and what we aspire to be.

Deep down, there is one final message in what took place in a backyard in Midland, Texas, for 2 1/2 days last week, and it is this: There is magic in believing — not the kind that is produced with hocus-pocus, but the kind that is produced through faith — and there is no greater a magician than a child.

Note: The rescue of the child, Jessica McClure, later became the subject of a television movie.

Reflections emerge as 50 arrives

Wabash Plain Dealer, Jan. 6, 1988

When your boss and your doctor both compliment you, along with lots of readers, you figure that you've written a pretty decent column — like this one.

They thought they were being real pals to me, those three friends, when they took me out for a celebratory beer on my 21st birthday. They knew I did not drink, but it did not matter. What they did not know — and it wouldn't have mattered either — was that turning 21 was no big deal to me.

When I turned 30, I laughed at the line, "You can't trust anyone over 30," and went on with my life, newly married and steeped in my first editorship.

At 40, I thought briefly — 12 minutes or so — about life "just beginning" and simply went about my business.

Age has never concerned me.

It still didn't as I turned 50 on Sunday. But as the half-century mark approached, I couldn't help but pause and reflect on where I have been, what I have seen, how my thinking has been shaped and what's important in the dessert days ahead.

The most important thing I have learned is that without a sense of values, our lives are empty.

Values change as our lives take twists and turns, but some ought to remain constant, embedded in our souls.

One such value is that we should constantly strive to do the right thing. So simple a thought. And yet, because we are not perfect beings, we fail at times, not deliberately, but because what we truly thought was right was simply wrong.

If we constantly remind ourselves to avoid doing anything immoral, illegal or unethical, doing the right thing will come naturally.

If one values doing the right thing, one finds peace of mind — another value.

Peace of mind is like a train. As long as it runs smoothly, not necessarily swiftly, it will reach its destination with a minimum of trouble. If the train derails, all sorts of problems are suddenly present.

When we have peace of mind, our lives don't derail. They run smoothly — yes, a little bumpy at times — and proceed forward toward achieving goals and ambitions that result in self-satisfaction, which is the most important satisfaction of all.

Another value comes into play here: mental toughness — staying focused on a problem when solutions are elusive. A strong sense of objectivity is needed, along with maintaining control of one's emotions.

The values I have noted thus far provide the foundation for a value we give little, if any, thought to when we are young, but ought to grow considerably by the time we reach adulthood.

I am talking about health, both mental and physical. Too many people take health for granted or fool themselves. The person who brags about not smoking may be 25 pounds overweight. My great sin is that I don't exercise enough, which bothers me because I make sure that I get plenty of rest and work at eating sanely while shunning tobacco and liquor.

Mental health, I believe, can be enhanced by another value — education. When the mind stops growing, the mind is in trouble. And an open mind is as important as a growing mind — indeed, contributes to growth. A closed mind can result in anathema: hypocrisy.

If we are frequently hypocritical, we cannot possess a value that our parents should begin developing in us the day we are born and should always remain at our core: the love of mankind.

We all possess a degree of selfishness, but if we love mankind, we not only contribute to the betterment of our society and our community, but to the mental health I noted earlier.

Let me take note of my parents here, to make a point. They

developed in me, my brother and sisters much more than the love of mankind. They were unable to give us much more than the basics in life, but they always made the holidays a happy time, and —much more importantly — provided the kind of stability so essential for children in their formative years.

Clearly, the foundation of my value system today comes from what my parents instilled in me in the formative years. And yet, I don't remember them doing anything special to get across their messages. They simply *cared*, and that's really all they needed to do.

And speaking of caring, that gets me to freedom, a value too many of us take for granted in this country. We fail to vote. We fail to attend meetings on social issues. We fail to visit on parent-teacher night. We fail to become involved in our communities.

Much of our problems — if not the majority of them — are caused by something too many of us value too much: money.

Of course money is important; we would be foolish not to value it. But when we place too much value on it our other values are endangered. If we work, work, work to get, get, get, we put the value of health on the line.

Hard work is fine — the work ethic ought to be a value that never ceases in us — but if we don't play, our mental health is threatened.

What I have come to understand clearly in the past 50 years is that the word "balance" is one of the simplest, yet most important, ones in our vocabulary. If we constantly strive for balance in a variety of diverse ways — in our diet, in presenting both sides of a controversy, in mixing work and play — we reduce our odds of becoming derailed.

Another simple word packed with importance is "tolerance." Like balance, it's not always easy to achieve. But if we keep that open mind I mentioned earlier, we improve our chances immensely.

Life is unfair, I have been told and have told others. I have seen much unfairness in the half-century past.

But life is wonderful, too, in our own little ways.

For every "jungle" out there, a piece of beauty can be ours — in the simplicity of an autumn day or neighbors helping a stricken farmer harvest the crop or watching the Special Olympics or taking in a parade or spotting grandma and grandpa hugging in the park.

For every sound of death and despair out there, a myriad of wonderful sounds can be ours — in Nat Cole singing "Stardust" or birds tweeting or a child's laughter or friends jiving over pizza and brew or the crack of a bat on a July afternoon or a gurgling brook.

For every "rotten apple" out there, dozens of Hank Leanders or Phil Cramers or Marge Gillespies or Marilyn Fords or Joe Nixons or Jim Engels or Hope Riders or Martha Joneses are around to brighten the day.

If I have sounded a bit righteous and a bit mawkish, forgive me. I did not intend to.

And as for my values — no, they aren't always perfectly in sync. But I can report that for the first 50 years of my life, I've had no serious derailments.

Which gets me to the belief in God — a value I am not comfortable talking about.

But there is no need to say much. One sentence will do: If He continues to watch over me as He has for the last 50 years, all the other values will take care of themselves.

Buckeye Bound and Beyond

From *Small School, Giant Dream, A Year of Hoosier High School Hoopla*

In 1990 I published a book about a small Indiana high school basketball team, Northfield in Wabash County, seeking to win the coveted State Championship. This was before class basketball — multiple titles based on school size — went into effect.

Northfield was led by a charismatic coach named Steve McClure and 6-10 and 6-9 twins Joe and Jon Ross.

A major test for the team occurred early in the season, when it was invited to play in a tournament in Ohio featuring top teams in the Midwest. This is the chapter covering that segment of Northfield's season.

The first gut-check of the season will take place on the banks of the Hocking River, which rims Ohio University at Athens to the south.

Steve McClure had hoped that his team could go into the McDonald's Days Inn Classic unbeaten before facing an unusually tough step up the ladder against Jim Derrow's Wellston, Ohio, Golden Rockets.

A step up the ladder normally means playing well and winning. Now, though, McClure feels another rung can be achieved even in defeat if Northfield plays much better than in its upset loss the night before at Tippecanoe Valley.

One thing's for sure: winning won't be easy. Derrow's team is 4-0, coming off a 70-58 victory four days earlier at Alexander High School, just up the road at Albany, Ohio. After the game, Alexander Coach Jay Rees told Kenneth Smailes of the Athens Messenger: "People thought Wellston would fold without (last year's District Player of the Year) Scott Bragg, but they haven't folded. They are just as good if not better."

Derrow launched the "Classic" in the 1988-89 season after having been invited to a similar event in previous years. Twelve teams participated the first year.

This year, he and five others formed a committee that narrowed a list of 150 teams to 25 before selecting the final 14, adding two teams and one game to the tournament.

The committee invited defending Indiana State Champion Lawrence North, which would be a particularly strong draw because of Eric Montross. But scheduling forced Lawrence North to decline.

Derrow had read about Joe and Jon Ross in the Street and Smith basketball magazine, and he liked "the idea of having All-American twins." So he called McClure in December 1988, asking about the Rosses and Northfield's program.

Once the 14 teams were set, the tournament committee worked out the best potential matchups. "We didn't put my team against Northfield for any other reason," Derrow said. "The way the teams stacked up, it worked out that way."

When the Ohio coach extended the invitation in February 1989, McClure wasted no time accepting. It would mean canceling one game to stay within IHSAA rules of 20 regular-season contests, and it could mean a long bus ride on top of another bus ride — from Tippecanoe Valley — the night before. But McClure knew the game would benefit Northfield's program.

McClure asked Athletic Director Jim Kaltenmark to reschedule the Tippecanoe Valley game, perhaps for right after Thanksgiving instead of December 15, but the matter fell through the cracks.

However, as game day dawns on a bitterly cold Saturday, a long morning/afternoon bus ride will be avoided. The Shirt Shed, a local firm specializing in printed T-shirts, has donated the use of its two company airplanes.

The planes seat six and eight, allowing Northfield to get 12 players and McClure and Steve Desper aboard. It is the first flight for some — including Desper.

There are a few ashen faces, including Desper's, at one o'clock as the two planes take off from Wabash Municipal Airport. Nervous or not, Desper has a sense of humor. He made out a will in his classroom Friday afternoon, bequeathing his golf clubs to various students.

A very nervous Brad Hampton slept fitfully, dreaming that the planes went down en route to Ohio. It was a vivid nightmare — flames, mangled bodies, "the whole thing," he admits. "You always hear about small planes crashing in weird planes with weird people on them."

But the pilot puts his passengers at ease quickly. Hampton and Nathan Winegardner occupy the pilot seats for a brief time, learning about radar and various controls.

Hampton's fears evaporate, and by the time the plane lands, he's thrilled with "a really neat trip."

Like Hampton, Desper relaxes once the plane gets airborne, prompting McClure to joke later, "Steve's talkin' about buyin' an airplane."

Fifty-three minutes later they are in Athens — full of excitement and flashing wide smiles. It will be another five hours before the Norsemen take the floor, so they head for the Days Inn. The motel chain has provided the teams staying overnight with five rooms. Sunday-morning breakfast will be courtesy of McDonald's.

After a short rest, McClure gathers his troops at 3:30 for a pre-game meal at a local restaurant.

Two hours later, the Norse leave for Ohio University to watch part of the game that precedes their encounter against Wellston. Northfield's contest is the sixth of the seven games, the opener pitting Ceredo-Kenova High School in Kenova, West Virginia, against Jay Rees' Alexander team. The final game has Cooley High in Detroit against Colonel White High in Dayton.

The Rosses will be the two tallest players during the day. And when they take the floor, there's murmuring in the crowd. "Look at those two guys," people are heard saying.

But the Rosses, like their teammates, are awed, too. There are only 1,000 people in the 13,000-seat Ohio University Convocation Center, but the facility's size has McClure's players wide-eyed.

Wellston's top player is Rob Hardee, a 6-5 senior who was an all-district and all-conference selection the year before for a team that went 20-4. He comes into the game as one of Wellston's four double-figure scorers, collecting 13.5 a game while pulling down nine rebounds. His scoring average can be deceiving. In this same event last year, he scored 28 points, while getting 19 rebounds, as Wellston lost to Columbus' Bishop Wehrle High School, 71-59.

But while McClure has to worry about Hardee and guard Chris Graham, Derrow has to fret about the Rosses. Three days before the game, he told Phil Beebe, sports editor of the *Wabash Plain Dealer*, "Their size really concerns us. You can't practice playing against size like that. We're concerned with playing them on the glass. We can't afford to let them get it and put it back up every time down the court."

Derrow, who scouted the Norsemen in their opener against Whitko, says he will try to counter Northfield's size with quickness. "We'll try to push the tempo every chance we get."

In the locker room, McClure, who is still bothered about his team's lack of focus in Friday night's game against Tippecanoe Valley, tells his people they have to "come back tonight and show that we learned from it, and that we're ready to move on."

He tells them to "chew up anything they throw at you. You didn't come down here to play in this arena just so you can say, 'Look at those pretty green seats.' You came down here to cross the line onto the court, and it's your opportunity to make the best of it."

Northfield fan buses were canceled because not enough people signed up — not because of the distance or sudden disinterest after one defeat, but because people have chosen to drive on their own. Later, Derrow reports that Northfield's pregame ticket sales far exceeded the other schools. So some 200 Norse rooters, most of them decked out in blue and white, are on hand.

It is a game they will never forget.

Like the previous night against Tippecanoe Valley, Northfield finds itself down early, as Wellston races to an 11-3 advantage. But the Norse put together an eight-point run, topped off by Joe Ross' thunderous, back-to-back dunks — one off a feed from brother Jon. A Wellston basket closes the quarter, giving the Rockets a 13-11 lead, and it's clear that this one will be a nail-biter.

The scoring streaks continue. Wellston rattles off five straight points to open the second quarter, for a run of seven. The Norse answer with a 12-2 blast, giving them their first lead, 23-20. And they cling to a 27-25 advantage at the half.

Northfield builds its margin to 38-33 in the third quarter. But Graham goes to work outside, Hardee inside, propelling the Rockets into a four-point advantage early in the fourth quarter. The margin could be eight, but Wellston has missed front-end free throws twice.

Northfield rallies, forcing two turnovers. And when Jon Ross scores, the Norse lead again, 48-47, with 2 minutes and 58 seconds left in the game.

The lead is short-lived as Graham hits a three. But Jon ties it at 50, putting back Nathan Winegardner's miss.

Mike Potts responds with two free throws at 1:24, putting Wellston on top, 52-50.

Sixty-one seconds remain when Hampton knots things at 52 with a 10-foot jumper.

As the seconds dwindle away in the final minute, Wellston holds the ball for the last shot.

Graham, who has hit four three-pointers, is open along the baseline — his favorite spot — and he lets fly. It bounds off the rim, no good. Winegardner gathers the rebound.

Time out, Northfield, with one second left. In the huddle, McClure tells his team to "go long to Joe." The pass is thrown and Joe makes the catch. He puts up a 10-footer. No good. Overtime — 52-52.

Twenty-one seconds into the three-minute overtime, Joe hits two free throws to give Northfield a 54-52 lead.

The margin shrinks to one at 1:28 when Potts hits a front-end free throw, for 54-53, but misses the second, and Jon clears.

Joe is fouled again with 41 seconds left, but he can't get the free throw down this time, and the ball goes out of bounds to Wellston.

The Rockets miss a shot and Jon grabs the rebound with 20 seconds left. The Norse crowd is going wild, seeing victory in their team's grasp.

But Scott Lackey makes a steal and converts it into a basket. It's 55-54, Wellston, with nine seconds left. Timeout, Northfield.

Winegardner inbounds to Hampton, who brings the ball up. Hampton feeds to Troy Miller. McClure has designed an offensive scheme that will produce a lay-up for Joe or Jon. But Miller sees it won't work. He dribbles to the top left of the lane, puts up a three.

Swish. Northfield, 57-55. There's no time on the clock.

But wait, Jim Derrow says, the horn didn't sound. He wants more time on the clock. McClure tends to agree.

"The clock showed zero, and the officials really didn't know what to do," he explains after the game. "Well, I had seen a situation like this before where you turn the clock on and if there is no horn, the game is over. But if you put it on and there is a horn, then there's still a second left."

After much discussion, the game resumes with one second, but Northfield doesn't allow Wellston to get a shot off. Northfield wins, 57-55.

"If we make our free throws we win the game," Derrow says afterward. "It's that simple."

And about the last second? "We thought they would go to Joe or Jon, and I think they probably would have if we hadn't sucked in so far. We knew after scouting them that Miller was an excellent three-point shooter. But you're going to take a chance. He hadn't hit any all night. If we're going to lose, we don't want to lose to the big kids."

And about the big kids? "They're just so doggone big, and we knew they would give us problems. They're better shooters than I thought they would be. Their shots were falling from 13, 14 feet. They handle the ball very well against pressure, and they make good decisions. I think when they gain some weight they'll be very nice collegiate players. They're very polite and hard-playing basketball players. You can't say enough about them."

And, as usual, they have led the way. Joe turns out to be the fourth highest scorer of the day with 23 and the top rebounder with 14. Jon has contributed 13 points and nine boards.

Asked to vote shortly before the game ended, the media gave the Most Valuable Player award to Graham when it looked like Wellston would win. But after the presentation, Derrow told his younger brother and top assistant, John, he thought someone on the winning team deserved the award and suggested Joe Ross. John Derrow agreed, and they approached Graham.

"I didn't force Graham to give up the award," Derrow said later. "I just told him our reasoning, and he agreed without hesitating."

So Derrow and Graham went into the Northfield locker room and presented the plaque to Joe. After Derrow and Graham's outstanding display of sportsmanship, McClure told his happy warriors, "That's a class act."

Then: "As soon as we left the (Northfield) gym last night I think Jon said something to the effect that we were going to come down here and have a good day. And as soon as I saw you guys at Ponderosa (for the pregame meal), you had your sweaters on and you came out with smiles on your faces. The sun was definitely up the next day and you had your heads high.

"You had to really block out some things to get it done. We didn't get the total weekend out of it. I really felt like we could handle Friday and Saturday. But we got on that plane this morning, our managers and everybody met us down here, we got to the hotel and there were Northfield people swarming the place.

"I just kind of thought, man, the day's been a success. Then you come down to overtime and I think, still, it's been a success. And there's nothing wrong with putting a little icing on top of it."

Miller is asked if he knew his shot was good when it left his hand. "Yes," he says. "I could feel it immediately."

Before the team showers and dresses, looking forward to watching the last game of the day, McClure tells them, "We're going to have a little devotional period tomorrow morning, since we'll be missing church."

Asked to reflect on the day, McClure says, "It was a good experience for us. We felt like it would be at the time we signed the contract, that it was something we could benefit from regardless.

"Wellston's a team that you definitely have to beat, because they are well disciplined, they play great defense and offense. They can play at any pace. Really, they're the type of team that we want to be or become. We had to beat 'em. They surely didn't beat themselves. I think they had somethin' like only 10 turnovers, and our defense had to force those. So we really feel good about what we accomplished.

"We needed a game like this ... with nothing riding on it. Well, I can't say nothing. But we just needed a chance to get out and have some fun ... and we did. We made progress, and that's the key."

And passed their first gut-check with flying colors.

After four straight on the road, the Norsemen are home for a rare mid-week contest, a conference game the following Wednesday, December 21, against North Miami.

The Warriors are 2-4. This one should be easy.

Outside, the wind chill is 51 degrees below zero. Inside, there's a warmth and coziness as another capacity crowd settles in.

The mood in the locker room is noticeably different as the players dress. The eerie silence of the last three games is missing — not replaced by boisterous behavior, but by a positive feeling of looseness. Perhaps the loss at Tippecanoe Valley and the win at Wellston have removed some early-season pressure.

There's less tension in the room as McClure delivers a brief pregame talk that's balanced between tactics and psychology.

"They're not a bad ballclub, guys," he says flatly. "They're capable of a great game — you just play a great game. We came back with a great effort Saturday. Let's not have the Caston syndrome. Let's not look for the 40-point win. Let's just play better. We've got to start feeling it like we did Saturday night against Wellston."

Joe Ross sinks two free throws after 16 seconds, and Jon follows with a field goal from in close 24 seconds later.

North Miami's top player, an outstanding guard named Brandon Fites, responds with a field goal. But Troy Miller comes back with three baskets, and at 4:47 it's 12-2. Tenacious defense is responsible for the quick lead.

It's 18-2 at 2:15 in the quarter when McClure goes to his bench, bringing in Winegardner and Noi at guard. The quarter ends at 24-8.

It's an old expression in sports, but it fits tonight: Northfield has too many horses. By the half, it's 40-14, and McClure has already substituted freely. He waits outside the locker room for a few minutes, "so they can talk among themselves. It's good for them."

"Keep it up, guys," Jon says. "Don't let up."

"No need to rush it; we're in control, " Hampton adds.

"Just like Oak Hill," Joe says. "We've got to get stronger."

McClure enters. "Everything works when you play with your bodies," he begins. "And you did a great job. You had good ball movement, exactly like the way you practiced this week. I love it! I love it! You've got a great evening of basketball goin'. We're playin' at our own standards tonight and they can't keep up. That's their problem."

But Northfield will not run up the score, McClure says. "We're not goin' to be pressin' as long as we're 20 ahead. They don't get any closer. We just build on the lead."

As the players warm up for the second half, Santa tosses candy to the kids in the crowd and the Northfield band plays White Christmas, seemingly in slow motion. It's a festive occasion for the home folks.

Peck Chay starts the second half with a short jumper off the glass from the middle of the lane, Joe follows with a semi-dunk and free throw, and Troy Miller pitches in with a jumper. It's 47-14 and the building process that McClure talked about at the half has begun.

The lead reaches 41, 58-17, on Hampton's two free throws at 2:09 in the quarter. North Miami's only score has been a three-pointer by Fites. A pretty reverse lay-up by Jon sends the crowd into a tizzy just before the quarter ends. It's 62-19.

At 6:19 of the final quarter McClure begins substituting, pulling the twins first. Scott Kunkel and David Pefley come in, and Kunkel, playing with his usual seriousness, goes two-for-two and grabs three rebounds.

But the other subs are a bit sloppy, allowing North Miami to score more points in the fourth quarter — 21 — than it had in the previous three.

It doesn't matter, of course. Besides, the crowd is getting a big kick out of Pefley, an excellent football player but average basketball player. A young man who doesn't take himself too seriously, Pefley was cut in his ninth-, tenth- and eleventh-grade years before making the team this year.

Now, in the final seconds, he scores from in close, bringing a huge cheer from the crowd. But he's not finished. As the clock dwindles down to five seconds, he gets a long rebound, dribbles behind the three-second line and lofts a trey. It's good. The announcer can hardly be heard.

The final is 80-41. In slightly more than three quarters, the Rosses have led the way again, getting 40 points between them, 23 by Jon. Joe has also picked up 13 rebounds. And young Noi Chay has played well again, collecting 12 points on four of nine shooting.

In his locker-room prayer, McClure says, "Father, don't let us mess up our priorities. We'll never be No. 1 because you're No. 1."

Then he tells his team he didn't like the last four minutes. "We had no leadership on the floor."

He wants them to have fun, he says — "Sure, it was a kill all the way" — but he doesn't want them to play well for only three and a half quarters.

Enough said.

The team presents him with a Christmas gift — a pen-holder for his desk, featuring a nameplate and a small basketball pole and hoop.

As his youngsters head for the showers, McClure walks outside to greet reporters. "We're startin' to put things together," he tells them. "What we're seein' in practice we're startin' to see in the games."

When defense is mentioned, he says, "Our defense has been steady all year, and we're goin' to keep improvin' it."

The Norse will need to. The two-day Wabash County Tournament starts in eight days, and while Northfield will be the favorite, winning the championship won't be easy. Two years ago, Wabash, which wound up winning four games all year, scored two stunning upsets to nab the title. And last year, with Northfield playing host, Manchester topped the Norsemen in a one-point overtime thriller.

But for now, McClure just wants to think about celebrating Christmas with his family and savor a nice rebound from the humiliating loss at Tippecanoe Valley.

Consolidation: where we stand

Wabash Plain Dealer, Aug. 8, 1991

School consolidation has long been a heated issue in Indiana.
In 1991, talk began about consolidating the Wabash city and Metropolitan school districts of Wabash County. At the time, I was publisher of the *Plain Dealer*. The paper produced an award-winning series of articles examining the issue.
The debate raged after I became editorial director for Nixon Newspapers in 1988, working out of company headquarters in nearby Peru. The *Plain Dealer*'s publisher asked me to write an editorial outlining the newspaper's position.

As the issue of school consolidation takes center stage again, we are prompted to make our position clear: we neither support nor oppose consolidating Wabash and Metropolitan school corporations.

The *Plain Dealer*'s position now is the same position it has held for several years: school consolidation should be discussed and studied by both school corporations.

We maintain this view despite the Metro board readopting on July 30 its resolution of May 1987, in which it said it "is not now, nor in the foreseeable future, interested in considering consolidation with the school city of Wabash."

The major difference now and four years ago is the likelihood that a referendum will be held to determine whether the two school districts should consolidate. We would have preferred a local fact-finding group study the issue and make a recommendation before such a referendum. However, since this no longer seems likely to happen, we hope both present their positions clearly and factually. We hope emotions and fears play little part in the referendum.

One thing that has not changed in four years is a perception that we support consolidation. We suspect that this incorrect perception is the result of past editorials that criticized the Metro board for refusing to even discuss consolidation.

Some history is in order here.

In the spring of 1987, the *Plain Dealer* wrote a series of articles on consolidation entitled: "School consolidation time again?" The series was written after the issue was raised in the community by some members of the Wabash Area Chamber of Commerce and others.

On May 12, after the series was published in its entirety, the *Plain Dealer* wrote an editorial that carried this headline: "Consolidation: let's take a fresh look."

The editorial recapped the pros and cons of consolidation brought out in the series. We said in part:

"Is the time right for consolidation?

"We don't know. But we agree with Metro Superintendent David Herbert, who, while not taking a position either way, said, 'I feel that I owe it to the future of this school corporation ... to say now is the time to consider consolidation."

Herbert was not saying he favored consolidation, and neither were we.

Within hours after that editorial appeared, the Metro board met and quickly passed its resolution. Then-Metro president Gary Nose expressed his desire to "(get) rid of the issue."

On May 14, the *Plain Dealer* editorialized again. The headline read: "Consolidation: it never got a chance." The editorial said in part:

"The *Plain Dealer* is not pushing for consolidation. It merely wanted (through the series of articles) to encourage a discussion by putting a wealth of information and ideas before its readers during its two-week series."

When the subject was brought up again in late 1989 by the Wabash City Schools board, then-Metro president Steve Peebles said he was "sick and tired" of talk about school consolidation.

In response to Peebles' comment, we editorialized again. The headline read: "Who's he speak for?" We deplored Peebles' outright refusal to even discuss the subject and the Metro board members' willingness to follow suit. Again, we did not take a stance either way on consolidation. If our response sounded like a personal attack on Peebles or other individual board members, it was not intended to be.

Which brings us to the present. In May 1987, we believed a local fact-finding group should have been formed to study consolidation. We still believe that now, but as stated earlier there doesn't appear to be time to accomplish that before a referendum in November. So now we are hoping that both sides put as much information on the table in a factual manner so that the voters in both school districts can vote intelligently, not emotionally.

As Jerry Ault, R.R. 5, said at the July 30 Metro meeting, the question is not about tax rates or athletics, but about what's best for the education of our young people.

And the question — What's best for education? — deserves to be answered by pursuing logical avenues. Consolidation is one of those avenues. It might not be the right avenue. But it ought to be at least explored.

Note: A referendum was eventually held. Consolidation was rejected by the voters.

Noble proves you can go home again

Peru Tribune, Aug. 24, 1998

This was one of the first freelance pieces I wrote after I retired in May 1998. I sold it to the *Peru Tribune,* the *Wabash Plain Dealer* and the *Bloomington* (Ind.) *Herald Times.*

Tim Noble, a native of Peru, had achieved international acclaim as an opera singer. At the time that I wrote this profile of him, he was living in his hometown.

He's a portly man who stands a shade under six feet, and today he's wearing a long-sleeved, satiny black shirt, denim-type black pants and moccasins with no socks. A thick, gray ponytail hangs between his shoulders flowing from a wealth of brown-gray hair that contrasts sharply with a trim, white mustache and beard. His cheeks are full, his eyes sparkle, and two native Indian-style earrings hang from his left ear.

It is shortly after noon and Tim Noble has arrived for lunch with the gang at Homer's, hard on the muddy Wabash River.

To his lunch companions, he's "just Tim," the guy who graduated from Peru High School in 1963, and, like others, left his small hometown 75 miles north of Indianapolis to find his life.

But to opera aficionados — from the Metropolitan in New York to stages in Paris, Amsterdam, Antwerp, San Francisco and Vienna, to mention a few — he's a baritone who has done it all in achieving international success and renown.

So what's Tim Noble doing in Homer's having the Friday special: fish fillets, fries and cole slaw for $4.25? Proving that contrary to what Thomas Wolfe wrote, you can go home again and savor your roots — that's what.

For Noble, the roots run from Peru to Bloomington, buried in love for native Indians, the outdoors and rivers. And then there is Donna, a hometown girl who became his wife some 28 months ago in what he describes as "a 24-7 marriage."

But four years ago the joy that Noble now exudes as he approaches 50 did not exist. On the contrary, he was depressed by personal matters, including a divorce that left him wondering what direction to take.

It was not the first time Noble had found himself in a quandary.

In 1977, he was in his second stint with Fred Waring's tremendously popular choral group, The Pennsylvanians, when the famous maestro asked him to take over the organization.

Between tours with Waring, Noble had performed in nightclubs, a Broadway production, commercials, pop shows in the Catskills and Miami Beach, and tours with the Hugo Winterhalter Orchestra. He had worked with Sarah Vaughn, Petula Clark and Doc Severinsen and appeared on the Ed Sullivan and Johnny Carson shows. By now, he knew that overseeing a group was not for him.

Still, he needed direction. So he called Steve Zegree, who was teaching piano at Western Michigan University and directing The Gold Company, a student group considered by connoisseurs to be among the top vocal-jazz ensembles in the world.

Zegree had met Noble while playing piano at music workshops Waring conducted in the Pocono Mountains.

"Why don't you go to IU and audition for the school of music to study voice?" Zegree suggested.

"When I heard Tim's voice," Zegree recalls today, "I just thought it was one of the most wonderful and extraordinary voices I had ever heard.

"I was doing a lot of accompaniment on the piano at Indiana University, where I was a graduate student. I thought that (Noble's) voice would lend itself really well to the operatic world, and Indiana is really the finest school in the world for training opera singers."

Still, Noble wondered about Zegree's suggestion. After all, he had been singing pop successfully for more than a dozen years. Then, again, he mused, maybe going back to school wouldn't be such a bad thing.

Noble's decision to leave the Pennsylvanians disappointed Waring, but did not anger him. Instead, Waring called Charles Webb, dean of the IU School of Music, who had once played piano for Waring. "Tim has a lot of talent; see what you can do for him," Waring asked Webb.

The dean responded by inviting Noble to opera auditions. With Zegree accompanying him, Noble sang, even though he didn't know any opera. "I just winged it and didn't think much of it," he recalls today.

Webb did.

"We've got to get you enrolled in this university," Zegree remembers Webb telling Noble. Never mind that the school year was scheduled to begin in two or three days. Webb wanted Noble to sing in IU opera productions and be assistant director of the Singing Hoosiers, which meant that Noble would have to be a graduate student.

But Noble did not have an undergraduate degree. He had entered Butler to study music education on a full scholarship, only to lose it, and he had left Ball State short of a degree to initially join Waring in 1968.

However, Webb worked things out, and in 3 1/2 years, Noble performed in 16 productions and learned to sing opera under the guidance of Eileen Farrell and Nicola Rossi-Lemeni, who had achieved international renown in their careers.

"Rossi-Lemeni had more effect on me than anyone I know, except my dad," Noble says today. (His father, James, had gained prominence as the music and band director at Peru High School during a 25-year teaching career before dying in 1972.)

"A voice like yours doesn't come around very often," Rossi-Lemeni told Noble. "You ought to do opera."

So Noble, who admits that pop is still his favorite genre, did. "When I got to IU, my voice was developed," he notes, "but I just didn't know it. It was just a matter of adding more power."

It was a matter, too, of learning how to move a lot of air through the vocal chords, master breath control and use the hard palette of the throat as a microphone.

In the fall of 1980, Noble got the break that would launch his opera career. Kurt Adler, the impresario of the San Francisco Opera, hired him, sight unseen, to sing *The Cry of Clytaemnestra*, based on Greek tragedy and just written by composer John Eaton. Several months later, Noble made his San Francisco Spring Opera debut as Agamemnon in Eaton's new work.

Noble was on his way. He appeared frequently with the San Francisco Opera and performed in other venues, winning kudos for performances in such roles as Rigoletto and Sharpless in Madame Butterfly.

By 1986, Noble was ready to make an important leap — to the Metropolitan Opera in New York. After a successful audition, he won his first role in 1988 in the Russian opera, *Khovanschina*.

What he had learned at IU about breath control and using the hard palette of his throat would be critical at the Met, which seats 4,000. "I can be heard better from the back than from the front," Noble points out.

Zegree, now a Western Michigan music professor and still directing The Gold Company, says Noble "has one of the great voices on the planet. What also distinguishes Tim from other opera singers is that he is a great dramatic actor-comic, too — and that's part of his success. One other thing that distinguishes him is he is a terrific musician (piano, drums, guitar). A lot of opera singers can't read music. He's got a great sense of pitch and rhythm and diction.

Using those talents, Noble spent 10 years, until this year, splitting his time annually. He performed for six months at the Met, then toured six months, both internationally and in such major American cities as Los Angeles, Philadelphia, Cincinnati, Houston and Dallas.

But while his professional career was booming, his personal life was hitting sour notes. He had lived in New York, San Francisco and on the Pueblo Indiana reservation in Santa Fe, N.M. In 1994, while based in Bloomington, he again was trying to sort things out. He called his mother, Jacquie.

"Why don't you come home?" she suggested. It had been 30 years since he had lived in his native Miami County. But just as he had taken Zegree's advice several years earlier, he took his mother's counsel.

It proved to be wise. He began a relationship with Donna, the vice principal of Peru Junior High School. After their marriage, he eventually adopted her children from a previous marriage, Ashley, an IU sophomore, and Kallie, who will enroll at Western Michigan in the fall to study music. And Donna eventually adopted Nikki, Noble's daughter from a previous marriage, who will be a first-grader.

While melding a new family, Noble has maintained close ties with his children from his first marriage: Nathan James Noble, 30, a percussion composer and arranger who lives in Muncie, and Kate Cole Noble, 21, a senior at Beloit College in Wisconsin.

When he's not away performing, Noble plays Mr. Mom, helping the kids with school, making beds, doing dishes, and cleaning around the house.

And each day he visits the Mississinewa River. "The trees are like being in a nave of a church," he says with a bit of awe. "It's like being in a religious place. I tell people that I go to church every day." A beefy smile spreads across his face.

"I'm a homegrown boy," he continues. "My mom and brother (Eric, an assistant golf pro in Fort Wayne) are here, and I don't worry about people hunting me down. It's quiet, and I can have peace of mind and just be one of the guys. In New York, it's helter skelter. I can be totally alone at the river."

When he's not visiting the Mississinewa, Noble practices at the piano, makes the Indian jewelry that he wears and reads voraciously, especially history.

And he gives himself to the community. When Lindsay Robison, a Peru Junior High eighth-grader, suffered a spinal cord injury, Noble took up Donna's suggestion of a benefit concert to help the Robisons with hefty medical bills. Noble recruited vocalist George Bowers and Zegree for the event.

Noble alters his routine as he prepares for a performance. He heads for Bloomington to work with Mark Phelps, a vocal coach for opera theater and a professor of music.

"Mark has been a good friend for many years and understands how I like to work," Noble says. "Something that might take six hours we can do in two because he knows me so well. I love to drive. I put my score next to me and sing and focus in silence."

Phelps' objectivity might be questioned, but when he's asked if Noble ranks among the top baritones in the world, the coach/professor responds with a brevity that gives his answer strength: "No doubt about it, he is among the very top. As you know, he performs year-round in all of the major opera centers of the world. The fact that he is hired with such frequency speaks for itself."

As well as Phelps knows Noble, Noble knows Falstaff. The title role of this Verdi opera has become Noble's signature portrayal and one of his two most favorite, the other being Iago in *Otello*. In October, Noble will do *Falstaff* six to eight times during its month-long run with the Tel Aviv New Israeli Opera.

He will leave for Israel in September, coming off performing in July at the Chautauqua Arts Festival in upstate New York. Before leaving for the festival, Noble prepared with Phelps for Donizetti's *Maria Stuarda* and Puccini's *Madame Butterfly*.

After performing in Israel — it will be his first trip there — Noble will appear in November at Clowes Hall on the Butler campus, doing Wagner's *The Flying Dutchman* in German.

As 1999 dawns, Noble might find himself being booked to perform again with his friend, Placido Domingo, the great tenor. They appeared together in a benefit in Puerto Rico for victims of the 1995 Mexico earthquake.

"I have as much respect for Placido from an artist point of view as anyone in the business," Noble volunteers. "He has great humanity. He knows how good he is, but doesn't go around bragging about it. He knows his place. I like that."

And now Tim Noble knows his place. His lunch pals at Homer's like that.

Note: Noble eventually moved from Peru to Bloomington, where he joined the faculty of Indiana University's prominent music school. He continued to perform at noted venues.

Highway of cooperation

Journal Gazette (Fort Wayne), Dec. 6, 1998

This piece was commissioned by the *Journal Gazette* for its Sunday Perspective section. It was one of the first freelance articles I wrote after I retired in June 1998 from Nixon Newspapers, Inc. In the Perspective section, writers have more latitude to analyze, interpret and use opinion.

Apathy draped another election — just 37 percent of registered voters cast ballots nationwide on Nov. 3, a figure that can demoralize citizens dedicated to the ideals of civic duty.

So for those people who despair over the lack of voter involvement, here's a dose of democracy: Outside the voting booth, at least, unity can overcome apathy — like along the Hoosier Heartland Industrial Corridor (HHIC).

What was merely a dream some 15 years ago has apparently turned the corner into reality (no pun intended), despite apathetic reactions and mumblings that periodically threatened to bury the idea.

The next time someone asserts that too many positive things fail because too many people are selfish and won't work together, point to the teamwork that has propelled the Corridor, a route about 115 miles long that's being transformed into a four-lane, limited-access highway between Fort Wayne and Lafayette via U.S. 24 and Indiana 25.

If the unity doubters have some spare time — say, three or four days — send them to Jack Porter and Glen Tanner. They proposed and pushed the corridor after the Wabash Area Chamber of Commerce saw a critical need to make U.S. 24 from Wabash to Huntington four lanes.

As Porter and Tanner studied the Wabash to Huntington link — about 17 miles — it became clear to them that this relatively small stretch was only one part of a much larger transportation puzzle, starting to the east in Fort Wayne.

Porter and Tanner began meeting with people in Peru, Logansport, Delphi and Lafayette. One by one, they formed a loosely aligned group designed to push for a Fort Wayne to Lafayette corridor, a seven-county route that makes more than just economic sense.

What has been remarkable from the outset is that while each community wanted certain pieces of U.S. 24 improved, self-interest has never raised its selfish head. Instead, the communities have pulled together as a nonprofit organization to put into place whatever piece of the U.S. 24-widening puzzle they could sell.

There were "a couple of slow years when a lot didn't get done," Tanner says, but never any major disagreements that threatened to seriously stall or threaten the project.

"We have meetings and get no nays," he continues. "Everybody says, 'We're for it.' We don't have somebody trying to put up a fence."

Porter adds: "We just kept pushing along. There was no end in quitting. We had to just keep working. It's been positive right down the line."

The efficacy of their all-for-one, one-for-all attitude is illustrated in light of the bruising battles that have stymied plans to extend Interstate 69. It is the only interstate serving the Fort Wayne area, running south from Port Huron, Mich., through that state's automotive sector before terminating at Interstate 65 in Indianapolis.

Plans to extend the route to the Mexican border have been delayed more than once as competing factions have tangled over how to proceed.

On Nov. 18, the state announced plans to broaden an environmental impact study, which will delay the start of any highway construction by 18 to 24 months — until at least 2003. When the impact study began, the project's cost was estimated to be $700 million. Now the estimate is $1 billion, according to Curt Wiley, commissioner of the Indiana Department of Transportation.

All of which is not to say that as the U.S. 24 corridor has moved toward reality, Porter, Tanner and others have always had a smooth ride. On the contrary, they've taken a roller coaster trip along the pancake-flat route, their hopes dipping and soaring, depending on the latest developments out of Indianapolis and Washington.

But the dips have always been cushioned in the seven key communities, where unity has stuck it to apathy. "Can't happen" has become "When it happens," and plans, paths and political partnerships have unfolded without pettiness.

The cement-solid cooperation has never cracked even as key government and business leaders have come and gone (and sometimes returned). Over the years, different individuals have served as:
- Executive directors of chambers of commerce.
- Economic development directors.
- County commissioners.
- County council members.
- City council members.
- Mayors. Peru's Richard Blair, elected in 1987, was part of a delegation that sought support in Washington. He was defeated for re-election in 1991, but he regained the post in 1995 and resumed supporting the project.
- Members of Congress. Republican Steve Buyer replaced Democrat Jim Jontz, and Republican Mark Souder supplanted Democrat Jill Long (who continued to aid the project as a U.S. Agriculture Department official in Washington). Nobody missed a beat.
- Governors, starting with the Republican Orr-Mutz administration and continuing through the Democratic Bayh-O'Bannon and O'Bannon-Kernan administrations. (When the project unfolded, Porter was a Wabash businessman and Republican activist who had played a key role in Dan Quayle's first congressional campaign. Tanner, also a Republican, was active in the Wabash Chamber of Commerce as sales manager for Wabash Metals Products.)
- State legislators. Republican Reps. Tom Weatherwax, Bill Friend, Rich McClain, Sue Scholer and Bill Ruppel and Sen. Harold "Potch" Wheeler have worked with Democrats Bayh and O'Bannon, especially the latter. Democratic Reps. Sheila Klinker and Win Moses and Sen. Michael Gery also have actively supported the project.
- Utility officials at NIPSCO and Cinergy, which was Public Service Indiana when the project was proposed.

Corridor-watchers might have needed the proverbial scorecard to keep track of the players. But the lineup changes didn't matter. Everyone working for a government or business team has sought the same victory.

Throughout this time, Porter and Tanner have been a guiding, glue-like force. They have stepped back only recently to allow others to steer the project to fulfillment, but they still attend meetings.

As the two men kept the Indiana political, business and economic entities together, the unity spread beyond the original corridor. An Ohio-based group gave corridor leaders ammunition by pushing a "Fort-to-Port" project that calls for improving the 81 miles from Fort Wayne to Toledo. Less than 15 miles of decent road now exist.

What is officially the Hoosier Heartland Industrial Corridor project in Indiana is now being sold to federal officials as the Heartland Corridor Highway. Fort Wayne is viewed as the route's central terminus, which gives Indiana additional economic impetus.

The Fort Wayne-Toledo corridor connects the Great Lakes to the nation's midsection — a natural transportation route for more than 200 years. The evolution of an Indiana project into a bi-state project means even greater benefits for Hoosiers as goods and services have wider potential to spread throughout the upper Midwest.

"Despite problems that have plagued it for two decades, America's manufacturing sector remains vital to the nation's economy," notes a 1996 study conducted for the HHIC. Prepared by William-Lynn-James Inc., a Carmel, Ind.-based consulting firm that specializes in economic development and revitalization, the study reports:

"Eighteen million Americans, one in every seven workers, are employed in the manufacturing sector. One-sixth of the nation's Gross Domestic Product is created in this sector. The heart of the country's manufacturing capability and capacity is found in the industrial areas of the Midwest. This region accounts for more than a quarter of the nation's manufacturing activity, more than 5 million of its jobs."

The Port of Toledo handles about 1,000 vessels per year, and Toledo is the third largest rail center in the nation, according to the Ohio Department of Commerce.

But the most important mode of transportation is the nation's highway network, sewn together by the Interstate system. With its heavy manufacturing presence, the upper Midwest is particularly vulnerable to inefficient road conditions, ranging from capacity to chuckholes.

And yet, until Porter, Tanner and others kept piping up, Indiana and Ohio officials didn't grasp the symbiotic Fort Wayne-to-Toledo link, not to mention the Toledo-to-Lafayette connection.

It's more than coincidental that starting in 1985, after the corridor idea began to blossom, significant employment growth began to occur over a 10-year period in Allen and Tippecanoe counties. Allen's workforce grew by almost 24 percent, while Tippecanoe's increased by about 23 percent, according to the William-Lynn-James study.

Since the early 1980s, the study notes, General Motors has built a sophisticated truck assembly plant in Fort Wayne, and other large manufacturing firms in the auto, electronics and fabricated metals industries have taken up residence, too. Meanwhile, in Lafayette, Caterpillar, Wabash National and Subaru-Isuzu Automotive have built plants.

But while Fort Wayne and Lafayette have been substantial winners, the smaller communities have maintained the corridor's HHIC's cohesiveness. Officials have recognized that by staying unified behind the corridor, their communities' growth potential will expand vastly through the economic interaction of companies, goods and people moving between Fort Wayne and Lafayette. For every $1 spent on the highway, the economic return is $3.50, according to the Indiana Department of Transportation.

In remaining united, officials have understood something else about the critical need to create a four-lane corridor: Safety. It is severely lacking in several places, resulting in traffic fatalities, serious injuries and destruction that translate into significant economic impact.

In testimony before an Indiana House transportation committee several years ago, Larry Hickman, who served 11 years as the economic development director for Wabash-based Wedcor, referred to the Huntington to Wabash stretch as the Ho Chi Minh Trail.

But the corridor project itself is not totally safe yet — not when an environmental impact study is about to begin for the Logansport-to-Lafayette segment. It will take about two years to scope out the archeology, historic landmarks, soil conditions and other factors — activity that the public does not see and that thus invites apathy.

However, ground was broken Nov. 12 for the $91.4 million segment between Huntington and Wabash, and work on the Logansport to Peru section has been under way for more than a year. The fact that people can see dirt being moved and cement being poured at two key segments ought to keep apathy buried.

And yet, the cement that has bonded business and government officials in the seven Hoosier counties will most likely continue to count the most, right up until the last dollars are provided by state and national lawmakers.

"The mantra of the people who have pushed this project has been, 'We want this highway; we need this highway,'" says William Bradley, Wedcor's executive director and secretary for the corridor's HHIC board of directors.

Which gets us back to Jack Porter and Glenn Tanner. When they first proposed the corridor, lots of folks said their dream was a folly that had no chance of becoming reality. Some people dubbed their idea as Noah's Ark.

If that's been so, a lot of people have booked passage over the years and proven that they can coexist.

Indy: The Most Adequate Spectacle in Racing?

Journal Gazette (Fort Wayne), May 30, 1999

This was another freelance assignment for the Perspective page.

Not long ago: A.J., the Andrettis, Emmo, the Unsers, Rick, Arie. Now: Billy Boat, Tony Stewart, Greg Ray, Eddie Cheever Jr., Buddy Lazier, Arie.

No long ago: accommodations booked solid before May, restaurant reservations tough to snag, race tickets at a premium. Now: accommodations available in May, restaurant reservations easier to nab, tickets floating around here and there.

Not long ago: Indianapolis is the place in May — sport, business and cultural diversity mingling for a month of *joi de vivre*. Now: fizzle in the festive atmosphere for the two-week event.

So the sun is setting on the Indianapolis 500 — "The Greatest Spectacle in Racing" — right?

Well, not so fast. But clearly, the 500 is not the overall racing event it once was. And like the Indiana state basketball tournament, the race may be becoming just another event, its tradition trashed by competing camps.

This year's race will be the fourth since the split between the Indy Racing League and Championship Auto Racing Teams, essentially triggered by Indianapolis Motor Speedway President Tony George. He has asserted control over an event that his grandfather, Tony Hulman, shaped into auto racing's No. 1 attraction.

George created the IRL in an effort to reduce the cost of competition, causing CART to pull out of the 500 and take most of the name drivers with it. Their absence has left skid marks on the event's image.

The race arguably will never regain its lost prestige — even if the IRL and CART repair their split soon. And arguably George has contributed to the 500's diminution through dilution. He brought NASCAR to the Speedway with the Brickyard 400, and he has booked the first Formula One race in the United States since 1991. It will take place Sept. 24, 2000, on a new course being built inside the Speedway.

People with an intimate knowledge of auto racing and those with only a passing interest indicate that while the 500 still holds its exultant place in sports, its prominence has waned.

As some people contend, dark clouds may be figuratively hanging over the new scoring tower as today's 83rd running of the 500 gets under way. But other people point out that the race is sold out again (which can be suspect, since the Indianapolis Motor Speedway never announces attendance figures).

Two men whose lives have been intimately intertwined with the race for decades — Dick Miller and Bud Freedman — reflect the dichotomy of disagreement over the 500's current status.

Miller saw his first race at the age of 10 in 1930 and has been magnetized by it ever since. From 1945 to 1972, he owned Dick's Men's Wear in Wabash, which for years gave away a suit of clothing to the 500 winner. It was big-time stuff for a small town when somebody like A.J. Foyt dropped in to get his duds.

Now, having done public relations work since 1984 for Provimi Veal, one of Arie Luyendyk's sponsors, Miller says: "The Speedway still has ticket sales in advance of one year and they're sold out every year. They're raising the price of tickets this coming year, 2000. They won't have a minute's trouble selling them."

Freedman was a high school student in Frankfort when he moved on his own to Indianapolis in 1961 and got a job working on the Dunn Engineering Special. The car didn't make the race, but a year later Freedman was a crew member on Rodger Ward's winning team.

"Today's Indy — it is seriously in jeopardy," says Freedman, who is now a gemologist. "The Internet is full of tickets at face value. Scalpers used to pay $700 for the B Penthouse. Indy is in a slow, steady decline, and I see no remedy.

"It's over as far as I'm concerned. I returned my application for a pit pass; they wanted $150. It's only an eight-day month of May. I can pay general admission, which is cheaper."

Jerry Miller, who wrote "Fast Company," a book about racing that was published in 1972, comes down somewhere between Freedman and Dick Miller (no relation).

Has the 500's time passed, he's asked? Jerry Miller, now a journalism professor at Franklin College, responds:

"I don't know if I would say its time has passed yet. I'm always hesitant to say that the race would ever die, because of the tradition and so forth."

But Jerry Miller adds that if there is no compromise between the IRL and CART and "stars, if you will" in CART don't return to Indy, "the path Tony George and his associates are down could lead to relegating the 500 in importance, if not extinction."

Jerry Miller believes the split "already has relegated Indianapolis to the second biggest race at the Indianapolis Motor Speedway behind the Brickyard 400."

Harold Chatlosh of Wabash, who has covered the last 42 races as a press photographer, doesn't see things that way. He agrees that the Brickyard 400 and Formula One at the Speedway take something away from the 500, but adds:

"The main race is the 500, and crowd-wise, it will never be beaten, because Tony George doesn't put up all the seats for the Brickyard 400. And he won't have all the seats there for the Formula One race. So that's why the 500 is the greatest spectacle in racing."

George pops up in almost every conversation about Indy.

"I have agreed and disagreed with him on some of the things he's doing," Dick Miller says. "But he is trying to help young fellas that have talent that can't come up with exorbitant sponsorship money to race and show their talents (which are) starting to surface. We've had some good boys that have beaten Arie and Roberto Guerrero, and some of these topnotch guys really stomped 'em around."

Says Freedman: "Tony George's three fatal errors were: the world of Indy car owners is much bigger than he thought. CART sponsors would demand they race at Indy. And the IRL has no money; almost all entrants are poverty-stricken."

Dave Tipton of Fort Wayne, whose strong interest in auto racing has paralleled a long career in advertising and marketing, says: "The 500 is not going to shrivel up and blow away. It will still be in existence for many years to come. In its same format — who's to say, other than Tony George."

Tipton continues: "Feelings that once existed can't be recaptured, no matter how hard one tries. There was a time, with TV blackouts on same-day coverage, when one felt special to go to the race and experience the awe and spectacle of the 500. I believe that is no longer a feeling experienced by many spectators. The heavy marketing linked with same-day broadcasts have hurt the race."

Jerry Miller, the journalism professor, cites the racing audience, too.

"If you look at the TV ratings, and so forth," he says, "everything seems to indicate that NASCAR stock car racing has become the most popular form in this country and is continuing to grow, whereas open-wheel racing, as in IRL or CART, is losing ground to NASCAR."

John Stackhouse of Peru, whose career has been in finance, thinks the 500's slippage centers primarily around Tony George and CART. But Stackhouse takes note of lifestyles, too.

Stackhouse, a strong race fan who was born and raised in South Bend, says, "I think today people probably have more disposable income. So buying tickets for the race, attending events, going out for practice, hanging over the rail watching favorite cars or drivers — it's all not what it used to be."

Stackhouse, a former Indianapolis-area resident, says the 500 once was the social event, especially for the business community.

He recalls when the first suite was built on the outside of Turn 2: "One of the tenants was Indiana National Bank. You used to receive invitations. The guest list was like the Who's Who of Indianapolis. It was all in a social setting, yet a lot of contacts and future business were derived from that setting."

But now the IRL-CART split "has significantly taken away from that whole aura," Stackhouse says. "The feeling's different. To me, it's just not the same."

Chatlosh, the photographer, touches on lifestyle in a different vein when accommodations are mentioned:

"You go down to Indianapolis now and look at the motor homes people bring in — at the camping and other stuff they're staying in. I think the motels got so high that people started to do other things to save some expenses. And since the race is down to two weeks, a lot of people come in for a weekend and drive back home the following weekend."

Mary Huggard is vice president of membership and development for the Indianapolis Convention and Visitors Association. Asked about accommodations, she alludes to the shortened race schedule:

"Although there has been a diminished impact at the beginning of the month, we're backloading at the end of the month. We're shifting people — there's more fluidity. We also have more rooms; we now have over 20,000 rooms available in our city."

As for restaurants, Huggard says, "There has been an explosion in restaurant experiences, too. Now things are spread out."

In the final analysis, the 500's status comes down to the driver question.

Chatlosh speaks for others when he contends: "The IRL and CART need to get back together, because the 500 needs more American drivers. You look at the name list now and you've got maybe 10 American drivers and that's it. Nobody knows these people."

Dick Miller thinks the two groups will, in fact, get back together soon.

"I'm more optimistic right now than I've been," he says. "When you take a powerhouse like (CART leader) Roger Penske that will openly say, 'I think it's time we get the organizations back together again' — when he is willing to say that, which he has done now, I think (a truce) could happen.

"It's a matter of a few egos. They've got to go. And I'm tickled to death to see Penske sell off some of his tracks, because he's awakened to the fact that we've got to save this kind of sport. I hope Tony George will take a little lesson from that and say, 'Hey, boys, let's sit down at the table again.'"

There are signs that this might be happening. Meanwhile, the Speedway has launched a marketing plan for the IRL that includes a 2,000 percent increase in advertising — to about $10 million this year.

A stronger marketing effort might have been organized even if the IRL-CART split had not occurred, because the Speedway no longer "owns" May. The basketball Pacers are in the NBA playoffs, and the Triple-A Indianapolis Indians baseball team plays in what might be the finest minor league park in the country.

The Speedway seems to be paying more attention to the media, too. Indiana editors received a letter that offered them two complimentary tickets. "We appreciate your participation in and coverage of all the racing events held at the Speedway," the letter said.

Jeff Ward, managing editor of the Peru *Tribune*, held up the letter and said: "It used to be that you couldn't get tickets unless you wrote for them. Now they're giving them away."

Ward, a dedicated racing fan who is not related to the IRL driver with the same name, then feigned a yawn. "But I'm not going this year," he said. "The race has lost its atmosphere."

Well, not quite. Jim Nabors will be back to sing "Back Home in Indiana," and native Hoosier Florence Henderson will warble again. And Billy Graham will offer the invocation, and gospel artist CeCe Winans will sing the national anthem, and "Tonight Show" host Jay Leno will drive the pace car.

And, as usual, thousands of colorful balloons will be released shortly before the 33 cars roar into action.

But too many of the best-known drivers won't be in those cars. And, after all is said and done, that's pretty much what the Indianapolis 500 is all about these days as the IRL-CART conflict drags on like the bombing in Kosovo.

Steel firm's dynamo

Journal Gazette (Fort Wayne), Aug. 22, 1999

Craig Klugman, editor of the *Journal Gazette*, called one day and said that his four-person business section staff was down to two reporters, one of whom was leaving in two weeks. He asked me if I would write six to eight major pieces for the Sunday business section while the paper went about hiring new reporters.

After I had written three stories, the business editor asked me to write a profile on Keith Busse, who had been featured with four other young executives in a business magazine.

The assignment turned out to be one of the most enjoyable I have ever experienced.

Keith Busse was pleasantly surprised when *Individual Investor* magazine chose him for its May 1999 cover, but what really thrilled him was the Jack Welch comparison that went with it.

Busse, the 56-year-old chief executive officer of Fort Wayne-based Steel Dynamics Inc., shared the cover with four other men whose thumb-print-size photos framed the bottom of the page.

The cover headline read: "Best Undiscovered CEOs. Invest in them. They could make you rich."

Inside, the text preceding the article read: "As CEO par excellence, General Electric's Jack Welch has made thousands of widows and orphans — not to mention money managers — rich. Our five undiscovered CEOs, who attack their jobs with the same drive to succeed as does Welch, could do the same for you."

The five men were chosen after the magazine conducted a search starting in December 1998, Executive Editor Alexander Haris told *The Journal Gazette*. "The whole premise was that management is important in selecting which company to invest in," Haris said. "Busse fit the bill."

Indeed, Busse is the central player in the "Steel Dynamics Inc. Story," the tale of a Fort Wayne firefighter's son leading a new company to immediate and growing success in an industry mired lately in hard times.

"I guess to be in the company of a fellow like Jack Welch is quite an honor," Busse said when asked about the *Individual Investor* cover. "To be compared to an individual with such stellar accomplishments is quite a tribute."

On a recent Monday, sitting behind his desk at Steel Dynamics's Fort Wayne headquarters on Pointe Inverness, the 5-foot-10, 210-pound Busse wore lightweight, khaki pants; a crisp, short-sleeved, forest-green Chaps shirt, and his usual tasseled loafers — casual dress that, at least on this day, could contribute to a fellow being undiscovered as one of the best CEOs.

Then, again, he's hardly been a CEO long enough to be discovered. It's only been since January 1996 that Steel Dynamics began production at its Butler plant, built for $280 million in an international record time of 14 months.

Still, analysts such as Waldo Best at Morgan Stanley Dean Witter express strong confidence in Steel Dynamics.

"SDI has the lowest cost structure in the United States, if not the world," Best said in an interview. "And because of that — even though a lot of the rest of the steel industry will not be profitable and likely lose money — SDI will become a shining star in an otherwise ugly earnings outlook. It is the only legitimate growth story in the steel industry."

In calling Steel Dynamics "a strong buy," Best said, "Its ... growth potential indicates that five to 10 years out, this company is going to be as big or bigger than U.S. Steel or Nucor.

"(Steel Dynamics) can offer a wide range of products, and they have proven themselves in quality certification. They gained ISO 9002 certification, which basically means that their quality has been benchmarked against the rest of the industry and found to be superior."

But Best is quick to note that Steel Dynamics is still a small company faced with how to grow its current 2.3 million tons per year. The top five industry leaders produce about 8 million to 11 million tons a year.

Since its inception, the Butler plant has achieved impressive numbers.

By the fourth month of production, the company was cash positive, said Busse, whose background is in accounting. "And in our sixth or seventh month, we were profitable by GAAP definition — accepted definition of a profit — which is as fast as any steel mill in history has ever turned cash flow or a bottom line.

"I don't think there's another steel mill in the history of this nation that's ever achieved a level of profitability in a six-month period of time."

What may be even more telling about the company, however, is its performance in an industry rocked in recent years by imported steel being dumped, driving prices down and leading to bankruptcies.

Steel Dynamics' success is an outgrowth of cost-cutting methods pioneered by Busse and others at Nucor Corp.'s Crawfordsville, Ind., plant.

As vice president and general manager for Nucor Corp. in 1987, Busse was assigned to build the world's first thin slab cast steel-making facility. By using state-of-the-art equipment and control technologies, he and his team developed production methods that slashed costs sharply, consumed far less energy and were environmentally cleaner.

"I think many people predicted that it (Crawfordsville) would be a total failure, a financial calamity for Nucor, that the product would be less than commercial quality," Busse recalled.

People didn't believe Busse when he said they would build the facility for about $250 million. "They believed that the cost of constructing a facility of this nature would approach 750 million to a billion dollars," Busse said, "because the standards in the industry were roughly a billion dollars of invested capital for each million tons of productive capability. The bet in the industry was that this was pure folly."

Busse and his team demolished conventional wisdom. In his Steel Dynamics biographical sketch, he notes that the man hours used per ton of prime steel produced at the Nucor plant "have been dramatically cut from the current level (February 1999) in the industry of approximately three to four hours to .55 hours." That figure has since dropped to .45.

Steel Dynamics has topped that kind of success at Butler. In the company's 1998 annual report, Busse wrote: "Our operating teams ... produced 7,000 tons of hot-rolled bands in a single day, and we are now producing hot-rolled steel for .33 man hours per ton."

Asked about operating profits per ton, Busse adjusted his wire-rimmed glasses as he said Steel Dynamics has recorded the industry's highest in eight of the last 10 quarters.

In 1998, the company achieved one of the highest operating profits — $50 per ton — in the industry on shipments of 1,414,950 tons, he told shareholders in the annual report. That was an increase of 211,703, or 18 percent, over 1997. And sales rose to $515 million vs. $420 million. A higher tax rate and the loss of tax benefits lowered the net income to $31.7 million from $43.9 million.

While racking up those numbers in 1998, Steel Dynamics added a cold roll mill, a new melt shop, a second caster and second tunnel furnace.

Those additions have helped push key measurements for the first six months of 1999 higher than for the same period a year ago. Net tons stood at 875,463, compared with 645,743. Net sales reached $284,114 million compared with $239,504 million. Net income was at $15,110 million vs. $15,089 million. Second-quarter earnings were $12.1 million, or 25 cents per diluted share, compared to 1998's second quarter of $7.5 million, or 15 cents per diluted share.

Waldo Best at Morgan Stanley likes Steel Dynamics' growth potential because of its management team: Busse, who joined Nucor in 1972; Mark Millett, vice president and general manager of Flat Roll Division; Richard "Dick" Teets, Jr., vice president and general manager of Structural Division; Tracy Shellabarger, vice president of finance and chief financial officer, and John Nolan, vice president of sales and marketing.

Millett and Teets left Nucor with Busse in August 1993. In April of that year, they had sat in an Indianapolis bar drinking beer and kicking around starting a new company. They scraped together $71,000 initially; by May 1994, after dealing with investors, they had $385 million, including financial aid from the state of Indiana.

Now, with Shellabarger and Nolan part of the mix, Best said: "The ability of (SDI's) team to execute is something that is very rare in the steel industry. It is the best five-person team arguably in the industry. SDI is probably one of the best-run companies in the United States, if not the world."

Best's praise might seem excessive, considering what Steel Dynamics's stock has done since going public. Steel Dynamics reached a high of 18 5/8 its first day of trading, Nov. 22, 1996. As of Thursday, Steel Dynamics stood at 17.

That number can be deceiving, according to Ronald Neuenschwander, senior vice president and branch manager for Wheat First Union in Fort Wayne.

Neuenschwander worked for McDonald and Co. when it helped Busse and his group raise the initial capital to build the Butler plant. And McDonald helped Steel Dynamics launch its IPO in 1996 that raised $150 million.

Asked about Steel Dynamics's current market standing, Neuenschwader said: "Many people ask me, "Well, I've held on to the stock for almost three years now, and it's gone — quote — nowhere. Why should I continue to hold it?' And the answer is that circumstances (dumped foreign steel) outside the control of the management team at Steel Dynamic caused the price to not be at what we anticipated when the stock went public."

Neuenschwander is buying Steel Dynamics stock for himself and "clients who have growth as an objective for an investment," he said. "I like the company long term very much. Steel Dynamics has virtually followed through on everything they said they were going to do from Day One."

Richard Aldridge, a steel analyst at Lehman Brothers, may

not have been as excited about Steel Dynamics as Best and Nuenschwander, but he is at least upbeat.

Aldridge, who finished second among 16 steel analysts in the 1998 All-Star competition conducted by Zacks Investment Research, termed Steel Dynamics "the upstart of the industry on the edge of technological breakthroughs. They can cast slabs to only 2 inches thick, instead of 8 inches thick, while still hot and roll it down with fewer workers and in less time normally required."

Aldridge echoed Best when he said: "SDI is a very well-run company with expertise that's not easy to come by. There have been lots of failures in the thin-slab industry. SDI is entrepreneurial; it has a lot of Nucor culture, which is a very lean operating culture — non-union workers, workers' pay based heavily on incentives and profit-related."

Busse exuded even more confidence. Steel Dynamics's numbers thus far this year would be even stronger, he noted, if the company's earnings had not been "impacted sharply by unfairly traded importation of flatroll wares."

Steel Dynamics participated with other steel companies in winning unfair trade cases. The rulings in the main, hot-rolled steel cases have contributed to a 27 percent reduction in imports since November. And U.S. steel prices have risen somewhat this year, according to the Associated Press.

Meanwhile, as the industry was gaining legal ground in court, Steel Dynamics was gaining economic ground with its Iron Dynamics Inc. plant, built next to the original Steel Dynamics plant in Butler.

Scheduled to open in December 1998, Iron Dynamics was delayed until March 1999 for a variety of reasons — from supplier problems to making sure certain field modifications were developing proprietary technology, Busse reported in the 1998 annual report.

Iron Dynamics is producing DRI — direct reduced iron — that, the company believes, when converted into liquid pig iron, will yield the best operating results of any virgin iron-making technology known thus far.

But while IDI was finally coming on line, Steel Dynamics's planned structural steel plant in Whitley County was running into delays. Two protesters — the United Association of Plumbers and Steamfitters Union Local 166 in Fort Wayne, and Citizens Organized Watch, a Columbia City group — have filed appeals with the state against the plant's air draft permit.

Construction scheduled to start in April may be delayed until October, Busse said, adding, "Obviously, we're going to be impacted and injured by that delay, and so we are concerned about it. But we're not overly concerned. It's not going to, in the end, deter us from growing the company in that particular segment of the market at that particular location."

There would be no Steel Dynamics and therefore no Whitley County dispute if not for a promotion Busse didn't get back in 1991.

As Dave Aycock was about to retire as Nucor's president, the company's CEO, Kenneth Iverson, considered two people to replace him: John Correnti and Busse. Iverson chose Correnti.

"Was I disappointed?" Busse asked. "Of course, I was disappointed. Did I think I was the better choice for the job? Of course, I did."

He was asked: If you had been chosen president, do we still have a Steel Dynamics?

"We do not," Busse responded without hesitation. "But we (Busse, Teets and Millett) didn't leave for that reason specifically. It was about opportunity. It wasn't about anger. Creating SDI was merely all about a business opportunity. And it was a chance to live an adventure. How many of us get an opportunity to live an adventure or a dream of this magnitude? Very few people."

Busse's wife didn't look forward to the adventure, he volunteered.

He recalled the time leading up to Steel Dynamics' creation:

"I had job offer after job offer. And for a period of time I really batted most of those offers aside and said, 'Geez, I work for one of the very best companies in the United States, not just in the steel game, but as a manufacturing entity perhaps one of the best-managed corporate entities in America today. I'm happy. I'm making good money. The company's making good money.'

"So why does anybody leave Camelot? That's the question my wife, at least, asked. She thought I was a lunatic for considering the creation of a brand new steel company, which became, in the end, Steel Dynamics. And I don't know that I could adequately explain it to her."

Busse's marriage stayed intact; his relationships at Nucor became, in his word, strained.

"After we broke away, they were not pleased, understandably. That is correct," he admitted.

Now, though, "We have a good relationship with Nucor. Mr. Correnti is no longer with Nucor today. (He resigned June 3.) So the industry is abuzz about the potential merger of Nucor and Steel Dynamics."

But Busse doesn't see it as a probability or likelihood.

If a merger occurred, though, another cover story would be a good bet. And Keith Busse's photo would probably be much bigger than the size of a thumbprint.

Cobbler is sole survivor

Journal Gazette (Fort Wayne), May 22, 2005

I needed new heels on two pair of shoes. The closest repair shop I could find from my home was about 30 miles away in North Manchester, just south of Fort Wayne. So on the way to the *Journal Gazette* one day, I stopped in at the place. My curiosity kicked in. The result was this story.

NORTH MANCHESTER — Backed financially by his father-in-law, Allen Selleck saw an opportunity 25 years ago to use his hands more productively to earn a living.

So when his early-morning shift as a ground-floor molder ended at the former North Manchester Foundry, he began spending two or three hours each afternoon learning the shoe repair business from long-time cobbler Fred Barnes.

"I'd seen this old fella make good money," Selleck, 49, recalls as he stands behind a small counter in his shoe repair shop at 214 E. Main St. "He had stocks and bonds, and, I mean, he was talking about how much money he had. And I thought, Heh. And I believed him, and I still believe him. I really do."

From foundry to footwear seemed like a natural transition.

"I'm good with my hands," Selleck says. "I think that's why I'm still here. I fix everything. Anything from belts, tool bags, luggage, jackets, purses, and that's what's in here now."

After six months of learning the trade from the retiring Barnes, Selleck bought Barnes Shoe Store, then at 108 E. Main St. It became Selleck Shoe Repair.

But what Selleck saw in 1980 — the neighborhood shoe repair

shop as a comfortable living — could be a metaphor today for the death of mom-and-pop businesses.

At least, that's the way he sees things, brought on mainly by cheap imports from nations such as China being sold in discount stores.

For proof, Selleck grabs a mailing he just received regarding a public auction of H&H Shoe and Luggage Repair Shop in the Colony Shop strip mall at 6427 Bluffton Road.

"See, here's another one," he says, holding up the four-page flier.

As more shops close, Selleck's place could become a shoe repair island that draws customers from several surrounding towns that lack such services.

But that's no consolation to Selleck, a rugged-looking man attired in the Western clothing he sells. Even with out-of-town traffic, he says, his business struggles to stay afloat.

Asked about his net income, he replies: "Might do $80,000 and end up in the low 20s."

Back in the early '90s, he did considerably better, Selleck says. "I think I made $40,000 one year," he says gleefully. "I was in seventh heaven. I'm not kidding."

Those years, however, were a fluke of sorts, thanks to Garth Brooks, the country singer who helped push the sale of boots and Western gear Selleck sells.

"Oh, man alive," Selleck recalls. "Even my teenagers were listening to Garth Brooks, to country Western, two-steppin', square dancin'. Schools started up. I mean it was just a big fad there."

Fads fade, of course.

"But you know, it made me feel good for a little while," Selleck says with a grin.

He says he felt good about last year, too, when he netted about $25,000.

But, he adds, health insurance and tax bills wiped out the $5,000 increase in business.

Meanwhile, his old, long and narrow building requires constant upkeep. Five years ago, he adds, the garage section of the roof needed $3,000 in repair work.

He hangs on, he says, because he rents two small apartments over his building, and his wife supplements the family income as a cook at an elementary school.

He has an 18-year-old daughter at home; his two adult sons are employed outside North Manchester.

"If we didn't have (the apartments), there's no way we could make it on $20,000," he says. "That pays for our mortgage."

Selleck believes "this world just kind of started going downhill for mom-and-pop shops and small towns when Wal-Mart and Kmart came in. Now, instead of having your sewing shops, your shoe-repair shops, anything that you used to go downtown for ... that's when they started dying, in 1980."

Selleck thinks that in 10 years, the only shoe repair shops will be in large cities such as Indianapolis. "Your small towns, it's over," he predicts.

That thought didn't enter his mind when his father-in-law, Paul Frieden, a fixture in North Manchester real estate, "took a long-haired, hot rod-type of guy and told him he could do anything he wanted to do. And I'd never heard that before, you know. Hey, somebody gives you a chance to get out of the foundry, you take it. And I did."

But now, as small shops like his fade away, he places the blame on one major factor: Cheap, inexpensive goods imported from China and other foreign nations that prompt people to buy new items instead of, for example, putting heels and soles on otherwise perfectly good shoes.

"That's the whole problem with the United States — imports," he asserts. "I don't care if it's the linen industry, the clothing industry. They're gone now. Ask anybody."

Instead of getting shoes repaired, he says, people "can get 'em (for) $15 at Wal-Mart or go to L.L. Bean. I've got some Chinese hikers out there from LaCrosse for, I think, $102. So anywhere from $15 to $102 for the companies that are having 'em made."

To compete with products being made in China, Selleck says, long-established footwear companies such as Wolverine and Red Wing are starting to make Chinese boots at $70, $80 and $90 a pair, compared with "the real Red Wings that cost $140 and $160."

After he started getting more into selling work shoes and boots, Selleck recalls, a customer couldn't come into his shop and find anything that wasn't made in America, "unless it was that stupid little saddle over there for $7 that I got from Mexico."

But if he had continued an "America only" philosophy, he adds, "I would have been out of business a long time ago. People want that $50 pair of boots. People want that $8 belt."

The Western gear is his savior, he says, accounting for 80 percent of his business.

But this aspect has evolved negatively, too, he says.

"I used to sell a shirt called Rockmount made in Denver, Colorado," he laments. "One of the first, best Western shirts ever. I don't carry (it) anymore. And I would love to."

Too expensive?

"Yeah. It's 40, 50 bucks for a shirt." He points to a rack. "I can sell these shirts for $19.90; nice Western shirts."

Asked how many pairs of shoes he repairs on an average day, Selleck responds: "You know, I was thinking about that earlier. When I first got in business, I could do 20, 25 pairs of soles or heels a week. Now I'm lucky to do six, five, four a week."

He says an out-of-county customer recently asked whether he could get new heels on two pairs of shoes while he waited.

Yes, Selleck replied, but the charge would be $2 extra — a total of $14 for each pair.

"I don't care anymore," he says, alluding to the extra charge for immediate service. "I really don't. If I don't sell retail to a guy, I'm not in this store. The repair is just that cherry on top."

Helen Levy at the H&H Shoe & Luggage Repair Shop echoes Selleck's comments about foreign goods.

"Imports are running everybody out of business," she asserts. "We can't compete with China."

(The May 9 edition of *Newsweek* magazine reported that Wal-Mart imported $18 billion worth of goods from China in 2004. The magazine also reported that China manufactures two-thirds of the world's shoes.)

Levy and her husband, Kenneth Holloway, have owned the shop for six years. The previous owner had it for 38, she said.

Primarily because they "can barely pay the bills anymore," they put the equipment and inventory up for auction May 14. But nobody bid on it as a whole.

Now she and her husband are planning to auction the inventory and equipment — including some antique cabinets — piecemeal in four to six weeks.

Levy specializes in repairing leather goods.

"Instead of getting a strap fixed on a purse, people will buy 'knock-offs' for $4 or $5," she says. "They look the same, but are made of cheap material. You can buy a new bag for $8 to $10 at Kmart."

Although Levy and her husband are leaving the business, Selleck is resigned to hanging on.

"I'm not going to be able to retire," he says flatly. "What am I going to go do? And will that job be there in three months? Then what?"

Can anything be done to save the mom-and-pop shops?, he's asked.

"No way, no way," he responds quickly. "It's just part of life. People want cheap. They want throwaway. They want to buy it six times a year. You'd be surprised how many guys come in here and tell me they've been buying Kmart shoes — $30, $40 — three to four times a year."

So, knowing 25 years ago what he knows now, would he have decided to use his hands the same way?

"Well, of course not," he says.

And a tiny grin creeps across his face.

Debate rages as area jobs feel effects of widening economy

Journal Gazette (Fort Wayne), Sept. 11, 2005

While doing freelance work for the *Journal Gazette*'s business section in 2005, I suggested a series on how globalization was affecting Northwest Indiana. The entire business staff wrote several articles. This is the opening piece I wrote for the series.

Inspired by patriotism, you shop for an American-made car from a local dealer, but as you search the region, you find your task disheartening.

You discover that while lots of parts are still made in America, increasingly, others are manufactured in foreign countries to reduce labor costs and boost efficiency, leading to smaller price tags.

Then you learn that automobiles are merely a high-profile example of a movement seeping across the world—in all directions—intersecting with economic, political and cultural institutions in an inexorable meshing of markets.

Welcome to the world of globalization.

Fort Wayne academicians say it is a force that is significantly affecting northeast Indiana, the nation and the world.

In essence, globalization can be described in four words: No borders. No barriers.

In broader terms, globalization includes "linkage," "consolidation," "merging," "penetration," "integration," "interdependence" and "transformation" — all in reference to, as Pulitzer Prize-winning columnist Thomas Friedman of the *New York Times* writes, "enabling corporations, countries and individuals to reach around the world farther, faster, deeper and cheaper than ever before."

At Indiana University-Purdue University Fort Wayne, George Bullion, an associate professor in the Department of Economics and director of the Center for Economic Education, defines globalization as "the merging of economic and political interests of the dominant countries in the world community. It is not a movement toward one-world government."

When a consumer buys a product made in another country, Bullion says, he or she underscores that globalization is occurring economically. And the same holds true when workers lose their jobs because production is outsourced.

Pamela Kephart, dean of the Keith Busse School of Business and Entrepreneurial Leadership at the University of Saint Francis, says, "Geography no longer defines who we are, what we represent and what we are capable of producing, buying or selling. ...

"Particularly in the last 20 years, the globalization concept has emerged, grown and been sustained due to economic, political and cultural factors."

Lillian Schumacher, an assistant professor at the Busse school, says, "The availability of global markets for purchasing and selling goods and services has been found to equate to cost and/or time savings — both of which are key elements in meeting customer demand and maintaining longer-term alliances."

At IPFW, James Lutz, chairman of the political science department, says globalization "means the penetration of different societies and cultures by outside ideas, values and ways of doing things. ... China's opening to the West, including violent periods, reflects (an) example of globalization where outside values and ideas penetrated a society."

Some analysts contend that the world economy was globalized as much 100 years ago as it is today, according to the International Monetary Fund.

But the IMF says the term has come into common usage since the 1980s, "reflecting technological advances that have made it easier and quicker to complete international transactions — both trade and financial flows."

Globalization has spawned intense debate among organizations, politicians and social thinkers — some of whom, not surprisingly, have agendas — over whether it improves or worsens the standing of the world's people.

The debate can be complex, but essentially it revolves around two primary issues:

- Whether compelling economic and technological changes are improving or worsening people's lives.
- The effect those changes are having on the environment.

Basically, proponents assert that underdeveloped nations improve economically as globalization matures, while opponents contend that the gap between the rich and poor nations merely widens.

On the environment, opponents argue that it will suffer serious harm, while proponents say it will be protected by accords such as the Kyoto Agreement on climate change that was negotiated in Japan in December 1997 and took effect last February.

Definitions and debates aside, globalization now affects the average person in Allen County.

Bullion notes that the county has felt the loss of many manufacturing jobs to other countries, particularly Mexico under provisions of the North America Free Trade Agreement.

However, he's quick to add that Allen County has benefited from a few foreign-owned companies establishing operations.

Along those lines, Schumacher notes that goods and services are no longer "American or Japanese," citing the purchasing of an "American car" as an example:

"Some parts are made in the U.S., others in Canada and others in China, India or Peru, because it is most efficient to produce in this fashion, and the result to me is an affordable vehicle. All the participants in any market transaction are interconnected globally directly or indirectly. ...

"The fact that many businesses, even small businesses, can no longer count on national vendors to succeed in business is a direct correlation. They must look outside North America to get the products they need to get their end products to the customer."

Matt Faley, an instructor at the Busse school, says there are at least three areas that will significantly change in the global arena and affect the average Allen County resident:

• Workers will become more of a commodity. "No longer will the U.S. rely on its labor as a significant market differentiator. Instead, local companies will come to rely on foreign labor markets to produce, service and support products. That will leave local companies to focus on innovation, business expansion and marketing."

• Financial markets will become more uniform. The euro is the first attempt to standardize exchange, a precursor of financial markets seeking more uniformity to "reduce the volatility and risk in foreign currency exchange."

• The trade deficit that grips the United States should level out. "Once the balance of payments in and out of our U.S. market has occurred, a greater focus can be placed on strategic management issues."

The movement of workers into advanced countries, Bullion says, has created considerable strain on the social and cultural systems in those nations.

But Bullion believes that eventually a significant portion of people who immigrate to the United States could return to their native lands and contribute to their development.

It's a given that the movement of workers will mean jobs won and jobs lost.

"The real difficulty, of course, has been predicting in what fields the losses and gains will occur," Lutz says. "The United States is no longer isolated economically from the rest of the world."

Lutz notes that while some kinds of work can be outsourced to foreign countries, other tasks involve a physical presence, requiring people to follow jobs.

Trade is another given, but Lutz thinks other economic activity may be more important today. He cites such functions as investment, integrated global production, and all kinds of "trade" in services.

Dealing effectively in global commerce, Faley says, will require organizations — multinational and lone entrepreneurs alike — "to understand the complexities that international trade add to the operations. (Organizations need) to develop multicultural leadership teams and constantly learn about the new cultures in foreign markets."

Zoher Shipchandler, associate dean and professor of marketing and international business at IPFW's School of Business and Management Science, agrees.

"In order to be more successful in international trade," he says, "you need to understand different cultures. This applies to the Japanese, the Dutch, the Indians, to everybody."

Shipchandler, who was raised in Bombay, India, and came to the United States when he was 25, doesn't think cultures will disappear as globalization grows. Instead, he believes there will be "an assimilation, or some blending of cultures."

But Shipchandler says there won't be one culture worldwide — as some globalization opponents contend — and, he adds, that's a plus.

Kephart also stresses the importance of dealing with different cultures.

"Allen County is a county of entrepreneurs. Owning one's own business requires a globalization mind-set," Kephart said. "The key to managing a global organization is to understand, respect and recognize foreign cultures. This will require organizations to become more flexible and creative in managing their businesses."

She mentions two other keys to being effective:

• Identifying skills and characteristics of labor markets and using them to leverage growth, efficiency and shareholder wealth.

• Identifying nations' commodities and natural resources, which, she adds, some experts believe is now lacking in many organizations.

Another key will be the development of next-generation technological products, which Faley says is already being done by many entrepreneurs in Allen County.

These products are being designed for movement overseas to serve specialized industries, such as watch-making in Switzerland, Faley says.

"Or the local example of any automotive tier one, two or three manufacturing company that supplies to GM in Fort Wayne," he continues. "These companies are directly impacted by the ramifications of globalization on a daily basis in most aspects of their business relationships and alliances."

As companies rethink and reshape strategies in a global sense, workers need to rethink and reshape their futures accordingly, Kephart says.

"Unless the average person enhances his or her job skills through education," she asserts, "sooner rather than later, he or she will be out of a job and not equipped to find other employment, as jobs today require more of an advanced skill set."

But while workers can control their futures to some degree through continuing education, their futures may rest more with how political systems deal with globalization's challenges.

Much political conflict today in many nations reflects controversies surrounding globalization, Lutz says. While some leaders and factions oppose such aspects as migration, job loss, intrusion of foreign values, and new economic systems, others embrace them.

"It is highly unlikely that any political groups can prevent globalization from occurring, but it is possible to control the pace of globalization to some extent," Lutz says. "These political battles will continue in the United States and the rest of the world."

Regardless of the debate in Washington, globalization points to difficult political and social times facing the United States.

Lutz says the movement explains the anger of groups opposed to foreign values and ideas, including culture and religion.

"Native-born extremists have attacked foreigners and minorities in their frustration with changes going on in society," he says. "There have been examples in Indiana, in Bloomington, and such attacks can occur anywhere."

Lutz says globalization has been a factor in the confrontation over terrorism, aided by increased communications and transportation. "It is more difficult for the United States to stay aloof from world problems even if it wanted to do so."

And then there are ecological issues.

Bullion thinks that in the future, the environment will become an even more important issue as globalization matures. As evidence, he cites the Kyoto Agreement.

Lutz says environmental arguments today "epitomize the effects of globalization," noting that 50 years ago, global environment was not debated. "(But) today we are concerned about the possibility of global warming or the depletion of global resources or global population growth."

On balance, the academicians deem globalization as having and will continue to have a positive effect.

"By and large, it is a benefit to both the economically advanced and lesser developed countries in the long run," Shipchandler says. "It opens foreign markets.

"Americans have access to good, quality products at lower prices from all over the world. It definitely raises our standard of living.

"At the same time, in the less developed countries, there is more manufacturing activity to cater to the demand of economically advanced countries."

Several less developed countries, such as his native India, are able to provide not only goods, but services to the economically advanced countries, Shipchandler notes. He cites services in the area of information technology and call-centers.

"As the lesser developed countries become prosperous," he says, "their demand for products from the economically advanced countries like America will increase, which will result, of course, in more jobs in the U.S."

Like Shipchandler, Bullion sees globalization as being a beneficial process "that will have long-term benefits, with the long term being defined as perhaps 100 years or more."

Bullion also sees a major political benefit, saying: "As diverse countries come to understand their shared interests, the result may be a reduction in the level of hostility that has been in evidence throughout most of the world's history."

Kephart comments: "Because of globalization, the borders by which businesses seek to better manage cost are widely opened. Businesses now have more choices and can also expand to who and where a product is sold. This is seen as boundary-less competitive marketplaces."

But, in the final analysis, will the poorer nations close the gap with the richer nations?

The poorer nations are beginning to gain ground, Schumacher says. She cites China, where the average wage is equivalent to $100 a month, which allows the average Chinese citizen to live well. The situation is similar in India, she adds.

Lutz has a darker view, saying: "There is no obvious way for poorer countries to catch up, barring the discovery of important natural resources.

"Many different paths have been tried, and a few countries have succeeded — Singapore, South Korea, Taiwan, among others — but now there are that many more countries to catch up to. If there was any single, sure path to catching up, it would have been found by now."

Thus far, Asian nations have made the greatest progress through globalization, while African and Mideast countries have struggled, the academicians say.

Saudi Arabia is an exception to some degree in the Mideast, Kephart and Schumacher note, because of oil's effect on the country's economic structure. But culture issues have slowed the Saudis' progress, they add.

One thing's for certain, the academicians say: Globalization will continue to march forward.

"I believe globalization is irreversible." Shipchandler says.

Lutz says: "It can no more be stopped than the tide can be turned back."

The most important question now, Lutz adds, is how societies and political systems adapt to globalization's presence, the changes it brings and the challenges it presents.

A Journalist's Journey

Bulldog rises from ashes with city's help

Journal Gazette (Fort Wayne), Oct. 8, 2006

Business and government need to work together to achieve win-win outcomes. I watched this occur with a company in Wabash and suggested this piece to the *Journal Gazette*.

Before the smoke had cleared, there stood Jerry Ault, president of Francis Slocum Bank, asking John Dawkins what he needed.

His mind jumbled, surveying the smoldering aftermath of a blaze that destroyed his downtown factory, Dawkins had no idea.

All Dawkins knew, in the waning days of 1987, was that the manufacturing plant he built in 1985 — Bulldog Battery — was gone, the victim of a blaze apparently caused by a compound pot being left on accidentally at 400 degrees over a weekend.

But nine months later — with insurance money, a loan from Francis Slocum and a low-interest loan the city arranged through a state program — Bulldog would rise again to become what it is today: a prime example for how government and industry can work together to achieve a win-win situation.

Bulldog manufactures industrial batteries that are distributed throughout the United States and exported to Canada, Puerto Rico, Hong Kong and South America.

Sales have grown to $40 million annually, and yearly gains have stabilized at 25 percent, according to company President Norman Benjamin.

But on the night of Dec. 26, 1987 — Benjamin's 39th birthday —

Dawkins wasn't sure a new factory would be built.

Benjamin recalled: "Basically, John said, 'We can walk away from it, leave it as it is, or we can get back in business. It's your call.'

"I said, 'We're here. Let's get it done. Let's build it.' And that's exactly what we did."

Benjamin cobbled together operations inside an unused building in Urbana, just north of Wabash, to keep Bulldog alive until it could fully recover.

Now, almost 20 years later, the city and Bulldog have just struck another deal in a continuing series of agreements that have given the company economic sustenance, added to the tax rolls and created jobs.

In August, Bulldog received two 10-year tax abatements from the city, solidifying the jobs of 148 employees with a combined payroll of more than $4 million. The employees—85 percent to 90 percent of whom live in Wabash County — have an average hourly salary of $13 and can take part in profit-sharing, 401(k) and health and life insurance plans.

One 10-year abatement will be for construction of a 27,000-square-foot addition to Precision Battery Fabrication, a 54,000-square-foot entity that began operations in 2003 in the industrial park on Wabash's north side. In return, Bulldog has agreed to create and maintain 15 new jobs through the end of 2010.

The addition, projected to open next August at a cost of $625,000, will make tire racks used to transport product in tire factories. The racks evolved from Bulldog's manufacturing of trays that house batteries.

The city has also given Bulldog 1.8 acres for the expansion.

The other 10-year abatement is for equipment being added to the downtown factory that opened in September 1988 after the fire.

The birth and rebirth of Bulldog Battery — and its subsequent rock-solid relationship with Wabash — was made possible by a former mayor, the late Dallas Winchester, and Dawkins, who began his career in the battery industry at General Motors in 1954.

After eight years with GM, Dawkins moved around the industry as an executive for the largest battery companies — Exide, Gould and

C and D. As he worked in different areas of the country, he observed employees.

"I knew about Indiana people from the work I did in Attica for C and D," Dawkins, 78 and still involved in Bulldog, recalled in an interview from his home in Dallas. "What impressed me was the employees were a cut above people I saw anywhere else."

So when Dawkins, who had established Bulldog in a small Chicago plant in 1977, needed to expand his company, he looked to Indiana.

He had read an article in a Chicago newspaper that "showcased Indiana under (then) Lt. Gov. (John) Mutz," Dawkins related.

"What caught my eye was that there were industrial fairs (known as Hoosier Hospitality Days)," Dawkins said. "They had a nice program to attract industry to the state."

Dawkins drove to a fair in Indianapolis and checked into a hotel room — compliments of the state — knowing he didn't want to locate in a large city.

"I liked the working conditions in small towns," Dawkins said.

Winchester, a Democrat, was elected mayor in 1984 after a career on the fire department that included a long stint as chief. He did not meet Dawkins at the industrial fair, but he heard about Dawkins' scouting trip.

A likable, folksy, savvy guy, Winchester pounced. He called Dawkins.

"I went to Wabash and met Dallas, and I looked at the (former DataVue) building," Dawkins recalled. "We did some negotiating. We worked out some very favorable terms. They gave me a good mortgage. So I personally bought the building (68,000 square feet of manufacturing space) from the city, which had acquired it, and leased it to Bulldog Battery."

The city punctuated the deal by removing an abandoned railroad line and repaving the road, which made a dock more accessible.

And the city paved a backyard it was using to park municipal vehicles. Dawkins moved to Marion and brought in Benjamin, whose background was in engineering, to oversee the day-to-day operations.

Benjamin has been president the past 12 years. A native of

Kankakee, Ill., he and Dawkins met when Benjamin was a consultant in the battery industry and Dawkins worked for Gould Battery.

Dawkins and Benjamin developed a strong relationship, which has, by all accounts, manifested itself into a powerful connection between Wabash and Bulldog.

Unlike some alliances between cities and businesses that sour after incentives kick in, the partnership between Wabash and Bulldog got sweeter as the company recovered from the '87 fire.

After recapitalizing, the company became profitable again in March 1990, 18 months after the fire, Dawkins recalled.

Growing steadily, Bulldog requested and was granted a 10-year abatement in the fall of 1992 for a 7,800-square-foot warehouse on Water Street, near the downtown plant. The warehouse was estimated to cost $105,600 and add five jobs to the company's then-35-person roster.

That project was dwarfed in May 1997, when the city granted another 10-year abatement for a 50,000-square-foot warehouse on Water Street.

The facility was estimated to cost $500,000 and add six more jobs. By now, Bulldog had grown to 52 employees.

Six years later, Wabash and Bulldog consummated the deal on Precision Battery Fabrication with an economic package that cemented the company's future in the city.

According to Benjamin, a 2003 economic package included:

• A 10-year abatement on the 54,000-square-foot building.

• The city giving Bulldog five-plus acres in the industrial park.

• A $250,000 city incentive that would be applied to buying state-of-the-art equipment worth $500,000. (Wabash had received a refund of County Economic Development Income Tax money from an Anderson company that left the city.)

In return, Bulldog signed an agreement to stay in Wabash for 10 years, said Joel Stein, the company's Wabash attorney.

Benjamin recalled that then-mayor Arvin Copeland came to him with an offer of 16 acres for Bulldog to build Precision Battery Fabrication.

"I said, 'Well, I need to have the fabricating, but I don't need quite that much real estate. I'd rather see you make better economic use of the land.' "

This "made a world of difference," Benjamin volunteered. "That building was put up, and we put in the operations for the battery trays and chargers before the tire racks (evolved). We had (then) approximately a million dollars in that building and the equipment."

Benjamin said the cost of the project would have been considerably greater if Bulldog had to buy the land.

Precision Battery Fabrication added 25 new jobs per the agreement. Employment has since grown to 80.

In a news release the city issued after the agreement, Copeland — elected in 2000 as an independent before declaring himself a Democrat — said: "We offered an attractive package to Bulldog that I'm sure influenced their decision to build a new facility here. Bulldog has been good for Wabash, and Wabash has been good for Bulldog."

Copeland said in a telephone interview he knew Bulldog needed to expand. "I actually sought him (Benjamin) out," Copeland confirmed. "We offered the 16 acres not knowing what (Bulldog) needed. He said, 'this is what we need.'"

Copeland said the Precision Battery Fabrication deal was one of his top two achievements in economic development.

"Norm is definitely a business guy," he said. "We worked very well together."

That relationship helped secure another crucial part of the 2003 economic package: The city approved closing a portion of Water Street, which Bulldog said was necessary for future expansion downtown.

"Closing Water Street was the first step to grow Bulldog Battery in Wabash and maintain the corporate headquarters," Stein said.

Bulldog's downtown plant was hemmed in — partly because of limits on some operations — as opposed to its sister plant, PowerFlow Systems in Terrell, Texas, where land was plentiful, Stein explained. Acquired in 1999, PowerFlow, situated just outside Dallas, was suitable to become Bulldog's headquarters.

"No new significant jobs have been created in Terrell since then,"

Stein said. "All the growth has been in Wabash, and future growth will be in Wabash."

Bob Vanlandingham, a Republican city councilman who defeated Copeland for mayor in 2004, supported Bulldog's latest requests for city assistance.

Vanlandingham, who retired after 31 years in elementary education, the past 26 as a principal, said he took office knowing "we better work our fannies off and retain what (business) we have. We want new industry, of course, but we don't want to lose anything."

He noted that the city has generously helped other firms, too, including long-entrenched GDX, formerly known as General Tire.

"The city has to be competitive," Vanlandingham said. "You have to always be aware of companies' needs. If you don't work together, the community loses. There's got to be give and take on both sides so the citizens benefit."

Like Copeland, Vanlandingham praises Benjamin: "Working with Norm has been great. He dots his I's and crosses his T's and gets everything in order before he moves. If he tells you he's going to do something, he does it."

"This has been an ongoing relationship," Stein said. "And we've always gone out of our way to inform (the city) of what the future holds. We never surprise anybody."

The future holds promise, Benjamin said. "We will grow (the downtown plant) to be over 200,000 square feet under one roof before it's all done. Right now we're 133,000 square feet, to give you an idea."

Plans are being developed for a new oxide mill that will be built over the portion of Water Street that was closed. And, Benjamin said, the company has bought land next to the downtown plant for future expansion.

Bulldog will ask for additional abatements as plans for more buildings and equipment are finalized, Benjamin said. And the company will continue to be active in supporting the community.

"We've been more active in the community in recent years, the last, probably, 15," Benjamin responded when asked. "We support a lot of activities, like the Honeywell Center. ... We contribute to the animal shelter, things like that. John (Dawkins) is a big animal lover. So we donated money to help get a new facility put up here."

The company is a "Gold Level" member — among the largest financial contributors — to the Chamber of Commerce, Stein said.

Cash is nice, but from a Chamber of Commerce perspective, it appears that Bulldog Battery's alliance with Wabash has been worth much more than money to the county-seat town of 11,000 people.